# The Cricklewood Tapestry

# The Cricklewood Tapestry

## Alan Coren

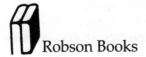 Robson Books

First published in paperback in Great Britain in 2001
by Robson Books, 10 Blenheim Court, Brewery Road,
London N7 9NY

A member of the Chrysalis Group plc

British Library Cataloguing in Publication Data
A catalogue record for this title is available from the
British Library

ISBN 1 86105 433 5

Typeset by FiSH Books, London
Printed and bound in Great Britain by
Creative Print & Design (Wales), Ebbw Vale

For Christopher Matthew

# Contents

# Introduction:
# A Twitch Upon the Thread

To look at me, up here in my Cricklewood loft, you wouldn't think I had much in common with an eleventh-century embroiderer. For a start (which is what this is), I am not stitching these words on to a square of linen with needle and thread, I am tapping them on to a square of screen with keyboard and mouse. True, my baldness is not dissimilar from his, but mine came by nature while his came by tonsure, and though we are both wearing thick brown robes with tasselled girdles, his indicates that he has recently got dressed, while mine indicates that I have recently got undressed. In short, he is a monk, and I am not.

Yet for all that, and for all that we are separated by nigh on a whole millennium, we are very similar indeed. For not only do we both work with life's rich tapestry in our twin continuing struggles to weave rich tapestries of our own, we are both working in the margins. He – *mon semblable, mon frère*, as he would murmur in his fluent Norman, were his plump ghost to be hovering behind me as I write – is working in the margins of the Bayeux Tapestry: he is not working in the broad sunlit uplands between the margins, those 70 shimmering metres of history's momentous warp and weft whose every stitch teems with political treachery and sacerdotal intrigue, with kings and noblemen alive and dead, with expansionist greed and bloody war, with, *tout court*, the big stuff of the Norman Conquest, he is working on the jolly grace notes above and below the major theme, the titchy figures going about their business of sex and cuisine, hawking and ploughing, planting and canoeing, aware, no doubt, of what is going on atop and beneath them, glancing briefly up or down, of course, at the serious players, but generally getting on with the variously fraught or cheering business of their own little lives.

And I, for my part, am working in the margins of the Cricklewood Tapestry. Ten centuries on, little has really changed: in the pages that follow, you will find, here and there, now and then, the major players of this millennium's passing show, whose doings inevitably brush against my own for good or ill, but mostly you will find all the little stuff that bobs along, as it has always done, in the big stuff's wake, to the tune of a penny whistle working its descants and counterpoints on weightier history's thunderous cacophany.

And one other tiny thing binds me, across the long arches of the years, to my marginal brother. We are both trying to weave as many laughs as life can muster. We are both doing our best to leave you in stitches.

AC

# Stands Cricklewood Where It Did?

RELUCTANT as I am to offer further confirmation to those of you who feel I should get out more – throw myself into cribbage or flamenco dancing, find a dog to walk, an instrument to master, a horse to hobby, anything rather than spend any more time woolgathering in my loft – I have to tell you (for it is my curse to do so) that in the summer of AD 97,999 it will be possible to dig for winkles on Cricklewood beach.

I worked that out after only an hour or so this morning. It is not, of course, what I climbed up into the loft to do, what I planned to do in the loft was have a bit of a think about whether President Saddam Hussein might not in fact be Lord Lucan. They are, after all, identical and of an age, and it would explain much. But while you may rest assured that I shall return to this theory at a later date, for the time being I prefer to nip forward 96,000 years to the time not yet being, so that I can trot downstairs from this loft, knot a hankie about my head, and go for a paddle. Because hardly had I begun investigating the likeliest fugitive route, in 1974, from Belgravia to Baghdad than a wheeling seagull suddenly shrieked outside my window, not merely raising my head from my atlas but also reminding me of a letter to *The Times* a week before, from the Chief Scientist of English Nature. I do not of course mean that it was the seagull's intention to do this, it was just an ordinary shriek, I mean only that my memory was jogged in that marine nano-second to the remarks of Dr Keith Duff, who had written to say that the recent erosion of Beachy Head was a natural force and we should think twice before shoring the coastline up with concrete, learning instead "to live with change rather than always seeking to prevent it".

What could a wool-gatherer do at this recollection but slap shut his atlas and phone English Nature in Peterborough? And yes, though Dr Duff was not at his desk, I did eventually get through to a helpful chap who could answer my question. The answer is that our southern coastline is eroding at roughly a metre a year. So I thanked him, I opened the atlas again, took a ruler, and noted that the distance between Beachy Head and Cricklewood, as the seagull flies, is 96 km. By AD 97,999, therefore, the sea will have reached my front gate Or, rather, 207 ft below it, this being my gate's height above sea-level, according to an equally helpful chap at the Ordnance Survey office. My house, in short, will be perched on the White Cliffs of Cricklewood, overlooking a charming little south coast resort.

Let us come down from the loft now, very slowly, three millennia a step, and look about us. See, my dining room contains not one large table but four small ones, each with a bottle of HP Sauce chained to it, and a jug of plastic cornflowers, and a cruet set engraved "Seaview

Boarding House". The walls once hung with pictures now sport framed notices: "Please Do Not Take Towels To Beach And Oblige" and "After Meals Ensure Your Serviette Is Replaced In Ring Provided". Let us, though, not linger, for a very slightly familiar bald man in a floral pinny has just come in to lay for lunch, and it is time for us to pop outside.

Oh, look, a fine summer morning, the sea-mist lifting to reveal Hendon Pier and the Edgware Lightship bobbing beyond, and the cheery strains of *William Tell* wafting up from the bandstand below, gilded gem of that fine broad promenade which stretches all the way from Golders Cove to Wembley Bay. Focus the big brass telescope standing on Seaview's fetchingly gnomed front lawn, and what do we see? We see beach huts, and whelk stalls, and ice-cream carts, and striped wooden deckchairs, we see little ones cross-legged on the sand hooting at Punch and Judy, and large ones wrapped in towels struggling to remove their trousers, we see pedalos and donkeys and a motor-boat rocking lazily beside a blackboard offering trips to Finchley Island ...

How reassuring it all is! How right Dr Duff was to urge us to live with change, for nothing really changes! Even though, as we step away from the telescope, a tiny piece of cliff beyond our feet breaks off, and falls.

# Legging It

I HAVE just been offered a horse's leg. This – since I sense your brow furrowing – is not a smart new cocktail, or a slap-up Belgian dinner, or even a Damien Hirst original; it is something a horse stands on. More precisely, something a quarter of a horse stands on. More precisely yet, something a quarter of a horse races on, for that is the sort of leg I have just been offered. The quarter is, of course, attached to three other quarters, because until genetic engineers come up with something to keep the Jockey Club talking far into the night, racehorses have to have a leg at each corner: at the time of writing, it would not be possible to run the Cesarewitch with what amounted to equine pogo-sticks, their jockeys hanging on to a haunch and the winner hopping in by a short rib. Though that, indeed, is exactly the sort of Cesarewitch I should like to see, if I were going to own a horse's leg: for it is being compelled to share ownership that is the nub of my present hesitation.

Because I am not sure if I want to own one quarter of a horse, when the friend who made me the offer will own the rest. He will have three quarters. Had things been different, had it been a matter of four men owning equal quarters each, the deal might have been appealing enough for me not to hesitate at all: we would have been D'Artagnan and the Three Musketeers, one for all and all for one, we would be marching as to war, or at any rate to Sandown Park, singing that we were not divided, all one body we, treating the imposture of triumph and disaster just the same, for just the same 25 per cent, divvying up the prize money equally, or sitting up all night while the poor thing coughed, stroking a leg each – but that isn't what I've been offered. I've been offered one quarter while my partner keeps three quarters of the four he presently has. I should be a minority legholder.

This bothers me. It bothers me because while I am not particularly interested in racing, per se, I rather relish its attendant bits and bobs. A sunny day out in a happily protected swath of England's rapidly diminishing greensward, the chance to wear Prince of Wales checks, and a brown fedora at a rakish angle, a shooting stick, a boutonniere, the ambience of glamorous women and florid chaps tucking into crustacea and champagne, a glimpse of the odd Queen and Sultan, the fluttered bob or two…I'm up for all of that, as indeed my friend well knew when he phoned and cannily played upon it. He guessed that I should fancy the notion of graduating from spectator to participant. He was not wrong.

And yet, and yet. How much of a participant would one become by dipping a single hoof in the water? True, I should be allowed into the pre-race paddock to mingle with the other owners, I should nod and chuckle knowingly like them, I might even tip my brown fedora to the odd Queen, but were she graciously to inquire which of mine was running in the first race, I should have in all honesty to reply, "A leg, ma'am," and this might puzzle her, she would glance at her race card, she would not find a horse called Aleg, she might put this to her trainer, he would incline and murmur, they might look at me, I should smile a sickly smile, and back away to seek my jockey – the one in my partner's colours,

5

except for one grudging panel, scant kudos there, it would be like having a Quarter-Blue for conkers – to ask him how things went in training, and he might say, "Hard to tell, one of the legs could be a bit iffy," and wink at his mates, for they are wags, jockeys, not slow to hoot and chortle.

And if it limped home last, what are the odds on every punter blaming my leg? Come to that, which leg would it be? A hind leg, and it would be more last than anything. I suppose I could insist on a foreleg, but, then again, suppose it tripped? And even if the whole horse won, what glory, in the winner's enclosure attaches to the jerk who is given the lid to hold, lest it fall off when the major legholder lifts the cup?

Time to ring him back. No need to tell him all I've told you. He's a well-read fellow, luckily, so I'll just say: four legs good, one leg bad.

# Curious Yellow

I BET you don't' know how significant a day 18 July 2004, is going to be. Indeed, I would be prepared to offer you any odds on that bet, if we had met anywhere but this column. Had we done that, and you had cared to commit yourself to one pound, I would have taken out a million of my own pounds and put them on the table. You would have had a bit of a think about 18 July 2004, you would then have given it your best shot, and I would have shaken my head and picked up your pound. But, sadly for me, this column is where we have met, and I cannot take your bet because this column is here for the sole purpose of telling you how significant a day 18 July 2004, is going to be, so all bets are off.

The reason I can be so confident of your, forgive me, ignorance is that I am also prepared to give you long odds that, at a little after 3 am last Thursday, you were not standing in your attic study on a piece of wallpaper 3 ft sq, tapping a pocket calculator even as you pored over copies of *Whitaker's Almanack* and the *Enyclopaedia Britannica* on the desk beside you. I, however, as you may have twigged, was, because I couldn't sleep and had trudged aloft to find a narcotic book; and since it was 3 am, I switched on the radio for the news before I ran my finger along the shelves. Thus, I was still listening and fingering when the radio murmured that China had just announced that its population, which had been increasing annually by 20 million, had now reached 1.25 billion. Can you guess what, a nano-second later, I wondered? Yes, spot on, I wondered whether all the Chinese could still stand on the Isle of Wight.

They could, the last time I heard. I heard it at Osidge Primary, when I was ten and the Chinese were 400 million. I had not thought about it since, but now, half a century on, I thought about it again. Far worse, I wanted to know.

But, at 3 am, there was nobody to ask. So I took down the *Encyclopaedia Britannica*, and found that the Isle of Wight covered 147 square miles. I then took down

*Whitaker's Almanack* and found that there were 640 acres to the square mile, and 4,840 sq yd to the acre. I then picked up my calculator; which after a bit of prodding, revealed that the Isle of Wight covered 455 347,200 sq yds.

All I then needed to know was how many Chinese occupied a square yard. I did not have any Chinese readily to hand, but I had bought a couple of suits in Hong Kong, once, and been told that I was regular size.

Assuming therefore that I was an honorary average Chinaman, that the average Chinawoman took up a bit more space, due to sticking out, but that the average Chinachild took up a bit less, it seemed reasonable, certainly to someone whose reason was beginning to crumble, that if I could discover how many of me could stand on a square yard, I should be nearly home. That is why I now went into the loft and cut a 3 ft sq piece of wallpaper from an old roll, and stood on it.

Having, naturally, first measured my width with a ruler. I am 2 ft across at my widest. I could not therefore get four of me on to my square yard. If, however, I stood triangularly, I could just fit three of me on.

I returned to my calculator because it was time to multiply 455,347,200 by three. The answer – though I'm sure you have it, too, because something tells me this is one of those columns where you are not going to let me get away with anything – is 1,366,041,600. That is exactly how many Chinese the Isle of Wight will bear. So I had my answer: the population of China, despite having risen to 1,250,000,000, can still stand on the Isle of Wight.

But for how long? Not how long can they stand there (although, admittedly, there isn't a lot to do on the Isle of Wight if you can't budge; 1,250,000,000 visitors would soon get fed up just standing), but how long will it be before the population of China, growing at 20 million per annum, cannot stand on it at all? I picked up my calculator again. Increasing by 54,795 per day, including two leap years, the last day on which, having reached 1,366,041,600, the population of China will be able to stand on the Isle of Wight will be 18 July 2004.

See how significant a day it has turned out to be? The next day, 54,795 Chinese will have to stand somewhere else.

# *Talk Is Cheap*

THE phone woke me up just now and said it was Tina Beatty here, and had I heard about Chatterday? I ought to have replied, "Of course I have, Ms Beatty, he is that useful middle-order batsman for Hyderabad, also bowls a bit, first-change seamer, safe pair of hands at second slip", rung off, and slipped effortlessly back to Dreamland. But I am not as quick on the blower as I am on paper, so I replied, "No, I haven't are you sure you have the correct number?" at which Tina instantly rattled off my number, and then she rattled off my name, and then, without drawing breath, gabbled eagerly on to tell me that she was offering a wonderful new service, and I thought, hallo, this is a quantum leap forward from cards in phone booths, this is girls in phone booths, if I don't ring off immediately Tina will be round with a folding bidet and a trunkful of clockwork prostheses, why me, I haven't left my card anywhere, have I?

But such was Tina's ticker-tape delivery that, before I could bang the instrument back into its cradle and snuggle down again into my own, she had launched into a complex narrative about astonishing telephone discounts of 33 per cent; whereupon I suddenly twigged that it was not Tina Beatty here at all, it was Tina, comma, BT, here, and that Chatterday was neither a sub-continental citizen nor a recherché sex aid, but a British occasion: it was a day on which I could chatter. More thrilling yet, it was, Tina rapidly revealed, four days on which I could chatter, each of them a Saturday in September, when for every paid two minutes BT would give me one more minute absolutely free; all I had to do to sign on was tell Tina whether I wanted to chatter between dawn and dusk or between dusk and dawn.

Dreamland having by now been reduced to rubble, I asked Tina why BT had decided upon this extraordinary benefaction, because I was curious to know what BT had programmed her to reply, and, sure enough, Tina did not say it was because BT believed that there was a sucker born every minute, she said it was because BT believed that Saturday was a day for long leisurely conversations – particularly with people who had not spoken to one another for some time – but that subscribers held back because of the cost. So I thanked Tina for her caring concern, and told her I should think about it. Which, quite literally, is what I have now trudged up here to the attic to do.

And it does not bear thinking about. For BT having used up all its brain cells on the tacky notion that by offering its customers a third off they would end up spending five times as much, had none left with which to consider whether they might, as a direct result, end up spending nothing at all. Speaking for myself, I shall not be speaking a word to anyone else on those four Saturdays. How could I? Since BT's enormous army of Tinas will soon have seen to it that all its subscribers have been apprised of their wondrous offer, everyone to whom I had not spoken for some time would be bound to conclude that I had not spoken to them because they were not worth three bob a minute. They were worth only two bob a minute. I should cry, hallo, it's me, your dear old friend, Alan, no, Alan, yes, one ell, no, Coren, yes, ha-ha-ha, only to hear the sound of a hand muffling an instrument so inadequately that the word cheapjack could not help but end up bouncing on my eardrum.

Furthermore, if BT is listening, it ought to know that I shan't be. Not only will I not call anyone on any of September's Saturdays, I shall not, if anyone calls me, pick the phone up. I do not care to discover that all the people who have not spoken to me for some time have finally got around to it only because I wasn't worth the money before. And the more I think about all this, Tina, the more I think that it is about something more than all this. Might BT have been deploying more brain cells than I gave it credit for? Is there just a chance that, guessing our fear of appearing pinchpenny, it has sussed that we shall, next month, so avoid making cheap calls that we shall be compelled to make only expensive ones? In short, has BT calculated that, if all goes to plan, 26 Chatterdays hath September?

# After You, Claude

To all those of you not so much reading this as holding it up to shield your frozen cheeks against the bitter wind howling down Croydon High Street or up the Great North Road, or round the Hanger Lane Gyratory, or wherever it is that the end of the Royal Academy queue currently finds itself, I bring great news. If you are interested in pictures of lily ponds, there is no need to spend the next few sodden days inching forward on chilblained feet nor the next few icy nights shivering in sleeping bags – simply hop on a bus, pop down the Tube, or hail a passing cab, and make for the Cricklewood atelier of an artist who, by uncanny coincidence, has, like Claude Monet himself, spent the past 26 years of his life not only obsessed with his pond but also immemorial-ising that obsession in a sequence of extraordinary pictures which chronicle the symbiotic relationship of pond and man with a clarity and poignancy which leave the old Giverny hermit at the post.

That they are in fact all photographs (apart from an exquisite wiring diagram showing how to install a pump powerful enough to electrocute goldfish) in no way diminishes their painterly quality: several, in their shim-mering focuslessness, in the famously quirky exposures bespeaking the artist's lifelong struggle to come to terms with the elusive nature of light, and in his unique trademark hand-wobble, call Impressionism indelibly to mind; while others, in their bizarre disposition of objects – a diagonal pond and tabby, half-masked by the artist's thumb, from his Cat-Next-Door Period, or *Man Sitting In Pond With Bottle And Chicken Leg* from his Sunday Drinks sequence, or the inspired double exposure *Gondola With Tadpoles*, created after a trip to Venice when the artist went into the garden to finish off the roll – evoke, of course, Chagall and Picasso. As for the terrifying *Pond With Artist's Wife Not Wanting To Be Photographed*, even Edvard Munch never came close.

Whence, then, this obsession? It began, straight-forwardly enough, in the summer of 1972, when the artist moved into the house, dug the pond, went down to Hendon Aquatics to buy half a dozen assorted lilies, and took the first proud picture in the collection, *Pond With Lilies*. The second picture, *Pond Without Lilies*, was taken to show Hendon Aquatics why the artist wanted his money back. *Pond Now Without Tree Keeping Sunlight Off New Lilies* was taken soon after receiving advice and more lilies from Hendon Aquatics, but led only to *Pond Without Lilies Again, Despite Chopping Down Tree*.

This marked the end of the artist's Lilies Period: inspired by Hendon Aquatics, he moved, now, into his Ornamental Fish Period, from which there are three pictures in the collection, the third being *Pond With Dead Fish*, a work which led a leading critic at Hendon Aquatics to make suggestions that ushered in the Cat-Next-Door Period, with the stunning configurations mentioned above – generated in part by the fact that the artist was now working more quickly, often running down the garden, snapping away to catch the cat at it. That he never did may be concluded from the evidence in the Sunday Drinks sequence, since the man in the pond is his next-door neighbour, with whom the artist obviously remained on good terms – despite the later *Pond With Kid's Football In It*, 1981, a lyrical still life followed a few weeks later by the charming narrative triptych *Pond With Wire Netting Over It*, *Artist's Daughter Testing Wire Netting*, and *Pond With Wire Netting And Artist's Daughter In It*.

Soon after came the artist's darkest period, when – following his gloomy study, *Pond Covered In Blanket Weed*, submitted to Hendon Aquatics, and a letter back saying they had no advice except keep taking it out – he got sick and tired of the pond, and stopped photographing it altogether. Indeed, great pains were taken to exclude it from his life as we can clearly (for once) see from the moving *Birthday Party 1998*, in which planks have been placed over the pond and a barbecue stood on them – an ironic comment, surely, on the ageing artist's feelings for what he had once dreamt would be a prime property-enhancing feature with top lilies, rare fish, and an electrically pumped fountain bound to bring guests rushing from every corner of his lawn to gawp and envy.

It was not to be; nor will it ever be, now. Peer closely at the final picture in the exhibition, taken a month ago, and you will eventually make out, if you are used to post-Pointillism, a nice new bench on a nice new terrace. It is not called that, mind: it is called *Former Lily Pond*.

# Game For Anything

IT will come as no surprise to you to hear that nothing comes as a surprise to *Times* readers. I have spent much of my life working among you, I have received thousands of your letters, and I know that when I glance at the sagging shelves of box files beside my desk, I am looking at one of the world's major collections of work by people over whom nothing can be put. You are not only bright as buttons but also worldly wise to a degree where, if there were degrees in worldly wisdom, you would all have firsts.

Thus it is I can be sure that when you opened your Monday *Times* at page 4 and saw the three items it comprised, you did not clutch at the sideboard for support, or call for a loved one to loosen your stays. A few of you may have raised your eyebrow or lowered your toast, but that would have been the top and bottom of it. News that a ban is being sought on a new titanium yo-yo, that red cards are to be used in the world conker championships so that offenders may be sent off, and that the nation's police horses are to carry sponsors' logos will not have turned a single hair. You will have said "funny old world", drained your coffee and got on with the business of the day.

Nevertheless, just this once something *will* have been put over on you, and because we go back a long way, you and I, I cannot allow you to remain unaware of it. Because what you will not have realised is that these three reports were not only covertly interconnected, but that, most covert of all, I was responsible for placing them there. I have contacts. You have to in this game, if you want to be a major player.

This game? Why, digital television, of course, the imminent advent of which means that anyone with what we in the industry call a sort of thing on the top of their sets will be able to receive several thousand new channels, of which Conkervision and Yo-Yo TV, having both been just founded by me, will assuredly be among the most successful, raking in sums in the neighbour-hood of pounds. For the nub of digital television is that not only will some people watch anything, but that at least three more of them will watch it if it involves sport. Particularly if that sport is in some way controversial, as conkers and yo-yo have just, it seems, become.

With this in mind, I have today signed up a major conker international who has already received two official warnings, one about pickling in vinegar and one about aiming at knuckles. As soon as Conkervision begins transmitting, he will, as per his contract, leave his radiant Dagenham common-law wife, who, while she may as yet be only a Page 7 Girl, does have a small, photogenic child by her former lover, a leading gobs cheat, and will herself be starring in my late-nite show, *Topless Conkers*.

All three, by the way are currently collaborating on a book of chestnut recipes, which will come with a full-frontal exercise video and a hit single by my new group, String. It should be noted that two per cent of proceeds from sales of Calvin Conker male fragrance in the five-litre tub will go to a charity close to Princess Michael's heart.

Since it would be unfair to make you, as old friends of mine, wait for the Sunday tabloid serialisation of the story of the woman the conker international ran off with, I am prepared to divulge that she is a leading yo-yo professional, star of my sister channel's imminently prime time *Titanium Tricks* and voluptuous model for the six new yo-yo away strips that my company will annually be retailing, in addition to a wide range of top-name forefinger accessories, diet chewing gum and, of course, ovenware designed with the yo-yo player in mind, in that all utensils can be carried in one hand, to avoid any interruption to attempts on the several records open to those who successfully match the celebrity face on that day's Yo-Yo TV scratchcard to the face on the Conkervision one.

But won't all this, you cry, cost a fortune to promote? Not with West Hampstead police stables lying at the top of my road. So if you soon spot posters drawing the attention of potential viewers and advertisers to both my wonderful new channels trotting about all over the place, it should come as no surprise to you.

# And I Alone Left Lingering Here

So, then, it is hats off to the Surrey Space Centre. Unless, of course, they are peaked. Those with peaked hats will not be doffing them to the Surrey Space Centre, because the Surrey Space Centre is seeing to it that those hats will soon be coming off for good. Any day now, their wearers will be trudging down to the local Job Centre, cap in hand. For the remarkable breakthrough which has earned my opening sentence means the end of meter reading as we know it: the University of Surrey Space Centre has perfected a technique for sending meter readers into space. But these are not meter readers in peaked hats, they will not whizz through the interstellar void aboard the *Starship Gasboard*, boldly going where no meter reader has gone before, they are titchy tin jobs called micro-satellites, and they will be able to read half a million meters at a single cybernetic shufti. Which means that the writing is on the wall for all those worthy toilers whose living has hitherto been guaranteed by the numbers on the wall.

This may not bother the rest of you too much: even the most humane among you will have felt a tiny tweak of selfish pleasure at the thought that you will no longer have to come home from the long day's graft to find a card on the mat telling you that you have been out, and demanding that you crawl into the cupboard under the stairs with a torch whose battery you meant to replace yesterday in order to peer at the numbers on the gas or electricity meter, jot them into the little boxes provided – with all the irritation consequent upon holding a card against a wall and writing with a ballpoint pen which doesn't like working uphill and goes dry halfway through so that you have to shake it, knocking to the floor the store of light bulbs you sensibly keep on the shelf above the meters – and then take them on the long walk to the postbox, only to have it suddenly strike you on the long walk back that you may have filled in the gas board's card with numbers you read off the electricity board's meter. Or, of course, vice versa.

But it bothers me. It gives me a no less selfish tweak, and mine is not pleasurable at all. For I do not come home from the long day's graft; home is where I do it, and, since Mrs Coren daily toddles off like you, it is a lonely place lightened only by the doorbell. Once upon a time, it would ping its way up here to the loft where I would be sat extruding words with all the enthusiasm of a man removing his own wisdom teeth, and at its ping I would punch the air, and hurtle downstairs, and fling wide the door upon this living being or that, often dragging them inside with one hand and putting the kettle on with the other. But then, five years ago, I lost the milkman to technological progress: agroboffins having ensured that eggs and milk and bread no longer needed to be fresh every day but could be super-marketed every week, the dairy stopped delivering, robbing me of the fellowship of Jim, three lumps ta very much, them chocolate digestives look all right, so then, what about QPR, bloody diabolical, what about this new wossname, lottery? Next, after the 1996 Budget, our

Shoreham fishmonger stopped his weekly London round, sorry Mr C, £3 a gallon, never mind cones all over, it can take four hours, it does not like hanging about, cod; and when, that same year, Barnet Council introduced the wheelie-bin so that I could push it on to the pavement myself, I lost even the brief hebdomadal joy of belting downstairs at the dustman's summons to share a fag break and exchange a graft-relieving word or two about the big-busted au pair opposite or the stuff I wouldn't believe them two old queens up the road put in their bins, I mean we're both men of the world, Al, but there's limits, am I right or am I wrong?

And now, thanks to the Surrey Space Centre, I am to lose, at one fell orbit, both my gasman and his electrical sidekick. Whom do I have left? Before very long, no doubt, the postman will not only not ring twice; he will not ring at all, because there will be no mail but e, the increasing bulk of newspapers will mean that the lad will no longer be able to deliver them since he does not have an HGV licence, and as for gypsies, Jack Straw patently stands poised to bang up all bogus fortune-tellers, they will no longer pop in to top up my stock of lucky white heather and have their palms crossed with silver for reading mine.

Which, I fear, leaves between me and utter solitude only the two cheery souls who stop by once a fortnight to deliver the latest *Watch Tower* and chew the theological fat. And I fear even more that I will not be left them long: any minute now, given the way everything is going, they will almost certainly be accessible only at Jehovah.com.

# Space Age

I am hugely cheered this morning. I have just discovered that, in only a few years time, I shall be able to do a 50ft-long jump. I shall be able to drive a golf ball a thousand yards. I shall be able to look at Cricklewood from a quarter of a million miles away.

I didn't think, until a moment ago, that I'd ever go to the Moon. I didn't think anyone would let me. Oh, sure, I've read all those articles about the imminence of lunar package tours – give it a decade and there will be daily jumbo shuttles ferrying holidaymakers to the Sea of Former Tranquillity, to be put up in Hecate Hiltons, gobble Gibbous McNuggets, camcord their infants as they somersault half a mile up from their trampolines, and excurse to the Dark Side in singsonging chara-buggies before shuttling Earthward again with their duty-free Moonshine and souvenir green cheese – but I'd never imagined I'd join them. To hurtle through space, you'd have to be young, you'd have to be fit, because nobody knew what might happen to wrinklies, out there.

Well, they'll know soon. I have just seen the latest *Vanity Fair*, which reveals that in January emeritus astronaut John Glenn will again be shot into space where Nasa will "conduct geriatric-related tests" to determine whether we senior citizens may indeed boldly go. And though the article does not specify these tests, experience has taught me to have a very good idea, which is why I am writing an article of my own. I am writing it for John to read, because I want John to pass with flying colours, so that I will one day be allowed to follow him.

For example, John, Nasa will make you take a spacewalk outside the capsule, to perform some task. By the time you get outside, however, you will have no idea why you are floating there. You will have forgotten why you went. Do not tell Nasa. Simply retrace your steps. Once you are back inside, it will suddenly come to you why you went outside. Once you are outside again though, the stars will look fuzzier than they did in 1962. That is because you have put your glasses down somewhere. Do not give the game away by going back inside to hunt for them, just perform your task, because you do not need long-distance glasses for close work. You need your reading glasses. Do not panic, they are on a string round your neck, remember? Wriggle your arm free inside the suit, put them on, do the task, climb back in.

The crew will applaud, and shake your hand. Thank them, but not by name, because though their faces are vaguely familiar, you will get their names wrong. If your long-distance glasses now float past from wherever it was you left them, catch them without comment. If your teeth float past, you have forgotten what I am about to tell you: each night, put the glass of water containing your dentures on the *underside* of the shelf beside your bunk. That way, they will stay there. Also take several empty bottles to bed: if you keep getting up during the night, Nasa will notice. They will also notice gravity's effect on your paunch unless you sleep face down. And don't pull ear- or nose-hairs out in an attempt to disguise age, these will float around and be remarked upon.

On waking, do not swallow your 14 different tablets for assorted geriatric conditions separately. This takes time, and when the crew tell you to get a move on for breakfast, you may instinctively shout back irritably. It is what old men do. Take all 14 at once, but also take care, especially if your hands tremble in the morning: a dropped senna pod could float around and be caught by someone who will ask about it. And here's a tip for when you put on your big beige cardigan: start buttoning it from the bottom, thus ensuring you do not go to breakfast with the buttons in the wrong holes. Nasa will be watching for tell-tale signs like that.

They will also watch you watching TV. Do not snore. Do not shout: "Why don't they make stuff like *Gunsmoke* any more?" Do not poke about in your ears. Do not ask for cocoa. Laugh at *The Simpsons*.

I do hope these little tips will help, John. Sorry there aren't more, I thought of some. I even made a list. Oh yes, here's another one: don't make lists. You'll only wind up asking if anyone's seen them anywhere.

# *Dolly Mixture*

I WAS ten when I performed my first abdominal operation. I exaggerate slightly: strictly speaking – which is what today's farrago is all about – I was ten when I *assisted* at my first abdominal operation. Roger Spenser was the surgeon, I was merely his house man, for Mandy was his patient: it was he to whom she had been referred by her distressed mama, because Mandy, not to mince words – which is what today's farrago is all about – had got into trouble. That is why she consulted Roger. His was the first name that came into Mandy's mama's head.

The trouble being that "mama" was not the first name that came into Mandy's head. It had been, once: once, her mama would pick her up, and Mandy would open her eyes and cry "mama" and her mama would change her, because Mandy was wet. But after a few weeks, Mandy stopped crying "maman when she was picked up; nor would she open her eyes unless her mama banged Mandy's head on the wall and, after a bit of this, she stopped opening her eyes at all. Also, she was constantly wet. So her mama prammed Mandy across the road to Roger's front garden, where Roger and I were fitting new brake blocks, and consulted him. Roger shook Mandy and diagnosed a leaking bladder. He could hear it sloshing about. His professional opinion was that Mandy's bladder was leaking into her works, mucking up her eyes and her voice thingy. He decided to operate forthwith. My job was to pass him the screwdriver and the pliers, and put Mandy's eyes in my pocket so they didn't get lost.

I have to say the operation was only partially successful. Because, after Roger had finished, Mandy's eyes did indeed open, but, having done so, they rolled around independently. That she appeared to have gone crazy was compounded by the fact that she did not say "mama" now, she said "erng". Despite this her mama (or rather, I suppose, her erng) seemed happy enough. She apparently did not mind that, when picked up, Mandy went "erng", rolled her eyes all over the place, and

24

squirted water out of her shoulder.

Which of course brings me to Furby. You will have read that Furby is going to be not only the hottest item this Christmas, but the most controversial item, too. For Furby is an animatronic, interactive cuddly toy made by Hasbro; he jumps off the shelf for £25 and he speaks 160 words. However, the words he speaks are Furbish, "a combination of Thai, Chinese and Hebrew", and thus a bit tricky to understand unless your child happens to be a Hassidic mandarin from Bangkok. So, as you would expect, the caring consortium has girded its loins for war, vanguarded by Sally Ward, head of language therapy at London's Speech, Language and Hearing Centre, who has told the press how very worried she is about the effects on the infant glottis from exposure to noises which make the Teletubbies sound like Brian Sewell.

Now, while I'm sure she knows whereof she speaks, and no less sure she speaks it beautifully, I beg leave to doubt the permanence of any damage inflicted by Furbish. I appreciate that Ms Ward, along with many a vicariously ambitious parent, would have preferred Hasbro to have invented, say, a Paxy, who would have deployed his enormous vocabulary and quizzical animatronic eyebrow to press his infant owner to answer umpteen penetrating questions before reducing him to tears and a scurry to the London Library; or a Melvy, who would daily convene a streetful of toddlers in their common, albeit contagiously adenoidal, search for a unified theory; but I fear that neither would last much longer than Boxing Day before having their heads banged against the wall, and not for going wrong, either. Because children, like the colleens in the uplands picking fraties, relish speaking a language that strangers do not know, and my guess is that, before long, they will have increased the Furbish vocabulary well beyond its present 160 words. I speak as one who can still speak ten times more Flowerpot than Bill and Ben ever flubberlubbed.

And the little girl whose dolly only said "erng"? She grew up to be a major headmistress. In educational circles, indeed, a household name.

# Servant Problem

IT was to have been a typically relaxed and jolly Bank Holiday weekend in the Coren household; and indeed, the Coren gardenhold, too, not to mention the Coren garagehold, for it was that time of year when this devoted couple traditionally leap up with the sun, canter downstairs trilling. "Oh, what a beautiful morning!" in perfect harmony, and hurl themselves into that vernal nest-furbishing which has characterised the 35 blissful springtimes of their union – he laughingly struggling up his wonky old ladder to prune the wistaria, she screaming caringly at him lest one incautious move bring her loved one tumbling to terminal injury, so touchingly close is the wistaria to her heart, she barrowing out the stored geraniums and dahlias from the garage, gently inquiring why the former are brown sticks and the latter rotted tubers, flinging the odd example at him for the informed horticultural opinion she so respects, he running off to clean the pond, she running after him lest he pocket the dead fish before he can tell her they have all swum to the bottom, they do that in May, she banging about in the shed looking for the new fork he hasn't bought and the gloves he inadvertently bonfired, eventually dragging the mower out backwards, because the wheels aren't going round, thanks to the annual service he didn't take it to in November, oh they are having such terrific marital fun, as anyone observing them would easily understand, once it was explained.

But this Bank Holiday they are not doing that at all. They are low, they are glum, they are worried, gardening is the last thing on their minds; for the newspapers were up with the sun, too, and are full of the tale of Tom Cruise and Nicole Kidman, another glittering couple no less mutually besotted than the Corens, who are under the cosh following the revelation that their domestic staff are forced to sign trap-shutting contracts on pain of millions of bucksworth of fines; because, claim the Cruises, staff could get the wrong end of the stick about marital discord, and run to the tabloids with their lucrative misinterpretations. Hence, of course, the wretchedness of the Corens: for they too have had hosts of minions over those 35 years, dailies and au pairs and general unhelps and jobbers of every conceivable oddity, few of them able to understand English words, let alone English ways; but it never occurred to the Corens to get the lawyers in first, and now it is too late, the world is full of loose cannons loaded and primed.

Oh, we do not fear the tabloid pounce. Holly and Crickle are rather dissimilar woods, but out there lie hundreds, perhaps thousands, of new employers who may well have cackled at the uninformed gossip of our treacherous ex-domestics. They may, indeed, be people we know, who now think they know us.

That is why I spent Bank Holiday not digging out weeds to give my beloved the satisfaction of identifying her new bedders, but in writing this piece to set the record straight. To rectify any misinterpretations that may be flying around. For how could an unsophisticated, albeit sharp-eyed, Kerry window-cleaner know that it has long been a custom among Cricklewood bridge players that, if their partnership has been heavily defeated for serious money, the partners will drive home and sleep in separate rooms, for no other reason than it gives each a better chance to rest undistracted after all that tiring fun? Show me the Filipino nanny who, sitting in the rear Volvo seat with her two small charges, suddenly hears a shout from the driver and appreciates that his wife has thrown the road map out of the window because that is how English-women demonstrate confidence in their husbands' navigational skills.

What chance is there of a simple Estonian daily understanding that finding a dismembered TV remote control in a wastebin means that her employers so empathise with one another that, rather than fall out over whether to watch the PGA championship or the omnibus *EastEnders*, they prefer to tune in to neither but instead do something both can enjoy, like phoning her mother and going out to clean his spark plugs?

And as for a socially untutored au pair, plucked from Umbria's bucolic innocence to wait at this bibulous dinner-party or that and spotting the animated attention being paid to the giggling divorcée on the host's left, how could she ever guess that the lack of conversation between her employers over the next few days was solely the result of Mrs Coren's solicitude for her hubbie's larynx, grown sore with all that selflessly hospitable banter?

How could she know that, unlike Tom and Nicole, the thought of getting a lawyer has never entered Mrs Coren's mind?

# *Smart Mouth*

Do you know where the toothbrush industry first went wrong? It first went wrong when it decided to become an industry. Once upon a time, don't ask me when, there was only one manufacturer of toothbrushes, and he was as happy as a manufacturer could be. He had a nice warm workshop where his cheery employees could stick bristles on to little sticks, and a nice clean counter where he could sell the little bristled sticks to the queue which, when it heard about them, began to form. Whereafter the queue became as happy as the manufacturer, because all it had ever dreamt of for its teeth was a little stick with bristles on, and now it had one.

However, as word got round and the rapidly lengthening queue exposed the market potential, new manufacturers set up in business; and since one bristled stick was much like another, they introduced variations, which they described as improvements. They were not improvements at all, of course, because any bristled stick does the job no better and no worse than the next bristled stick, as we – who have tried every catchpenny development which, down the subsequent years, the by now enormous toothbrush industry has thrown at us – know full well. For, whatever new bogus idiosyncracy of gum or chopper is conjured up, whatever gimcrack configuration of head or grip or handle is cobbled to address it, whatever brushing-edge technology is deployed on wondrous new materials culled from atoll or rainforest or space shuttle, the result is exactly the same. You wiggle a little bristled stick about inside your mouth until it is time to spit and everything inside your mouth is left in the same condition in which it was always left.

Which is precisely why it was all, from the very beginning, bound to go wrong: bringing unnecessarily complex industry to a necessarily simple craft could have only one end. That first happy manufacturer was the last happy manufacturer; they are all desperate manufacturers now. Bitter competition has seen to that, nature red in tooth and gum, and suddenly there is no new turn for the toothbrush to take. It has come to the dead end of its evolutionary road. I know this, because I have just been sent the newest toothbrush from a major manufacturer earnestly hoping this column will give him a leg up; but it will give him only a thumb down, because not only is his new toothbrush not new at all, it is exulting in the fact that it is old. For it is called The Classic, and it looks exactly like toothbrushes did when the happy manufacturer sold his first one. And do you know why it is called The Classic? It is because, according to the accompanying supergloss taradiddle, "here is a toothbrush with *style*".

So has it come to this? Even in this hapless designer-dogged culture, when the cognoscenti dare not be seen dead in last week's Armani shroud, what is the point of a stylish toothbrush? Who is going to be impressed by it, and, more to the point, how? Is the fashionable woman to poke it into her coiffe, where once she wore her sunglasses? The stylish man to sport it in his unbuttoned jacket-cuff, with just an inch of label showing? Are both supposed, at some swish dinner-party, to spring up half way through the pudding, declare they are off to winkle a rogue raspberry pip from their bicuspid, and flourish the thing in the air, for all to swoon? Should chic youth staple the new toothbrush to its nipples, or bulk each pocket of its cargo pants with half a gross? Will hotel managers fawningly upgrade your room, gratis, when the wink is tipped by the chambermaid that a Classic is standing in your beaker? Would it advance a business career if, at a crucial meeting, a briefcase were so cannily snapped open as to allow The Classic to tumble enviably on the boardroom table? Might the mere sight of it dangling from its bathroom rack be sufficient to rekindle a guttering relationship, or, glimpsed by a hitherto reluctant quarry when powdering her (or his) nose, ignite a new one?

Last question: why does this so worry me? It worries me because of a nagging fear that the answer to all the other questions might be yes.

# Power Sharing

I HAVE just switched on my computer to write this. And, I fear, plunged Burnley into darkness.

I fear this, because yesterday, when John Prescott urged the nation to counter global warming by reducing its use of tellies and computers, I learnt that "half a million tonnes of greenhouse gases could be saved, the equivalent of powering two towns the size of Burnley". And as always happens when statistics are simplified in the name of impact, they become only more imponderable: I can now think of nothing except Burnley, but having no idea what size Burnley is, and thus no idea of the damage my computer is doing to it, what am I to make of *two* towns the size of Burnley? Was it beyond the wit (sic) of Mr Prescott to come up with one town twice the size of Burnley, and more nationally familiar? Or is it that he is cunningly spinning the blunder of Eddie George – who would clearly sacrifice a couple of Burnleys in the metropolitan interest – to prick my Southern conscience about selfishly tapping my nonsense out while Northerners stumble around in the dark, banging their heads on things?

If so, he has no need to. I am a caring man, and even though I cannot visualise Burnley, neither can I rid my imagination of its citizens not only falling down its unlit stairs as the consequence of my keyboarding, but also being rushed by gas-guzzling ambulances to hospitals whose burning electricity could do such damage to the ozone layer as to precipitate the death of Earth. Had I been writing this in longhand, none of that would have happened. We are talking horseshoe nails here.

But, then again, which horse shoe nails? John says we can all help Burnley by switching our tellies off instead of leaving them on standby: but if you switch a telly off, you cannot switch it on again with the remote, you have to get out of your chair, cross the floor, and bend down, thereby burning umpteen calories which can be replaced only by food you will have to take from an electric freezer (making it work harder to compensate for its door being opened) to cook on stoves whose fumes could cause far more damage to Burnley and the Other Burnley than merely leaving a tiny red bulb on. Even if you have also switched off the cooker's pilot light and the electric push button in deference to Mr Prescott, because who is to say that striking a match and sending burnt phosphorus into the welkin is any less harmful? More ungraspable yet, my local Neighbourhood Watch advises us to leave a radio or TV playing when we go out, to discourage burglars; bad news for both Burnleys perhaps, but wouldn't it be worse if we didn't, and burglars got in, stole the sets, and sold them cheap to customers who had hitherto not been able to afford them, and then switched them on to black out yet a third Burnley?

Yes, he's a queer cove, your Johnny Energy: it is impossible ever to calculate the point at which more of it is wasted in saving than in using. Should I do my environmental bit by giving up my electric shaver, when, if I shaved wet, I should have not only to dispose of non-biodegradable blades, but also to get in my car every week to buy new ones? Is my electric trouser press more of a threat to Burnley than my steam iron? And if I used neither, but walked, caringly not driving, to the dry cleaner, who can say that he will not waste more precious resources than I by pressing them for me? Even if it were less, might my pushing the button to change the traffic lights so I could cross the road to his shop not defeat the entire enterprise? I shan't even chuck my worn shoe leather into this fraught equation, given that my heel bar uses an electric riveter, and the cow that provides the heels had to be dieselled to the slaughterhouse, and power felled. Unless, of course, John has ordered its owner to ride it there and hit it with a brick.

Enough of this, I've just totted up, that's 800 words, I can switch off now. And look, the lights are going on all over Burnley.

# Lemon Drop

IT is Armistice Day. It is a very big day indeed. It is the day I bring the lemon tree in. I do not, mind, bring the lemon tree in because it is Armistice Day – I do not, that is, bring it in as a private memorial pact, the lemon tree does not signify some personal ritual homage to the glorious fallen, it does not, as it were, commemorate a gallant grandpa who copped it in the Dardanelles, few poppies there, in Turkish fields the lemons blow, let us therefore wear the lemon with pride, place it in the hall, stand silently beside it between 11 am and 11.02. It has nothing to do with any of that: I bring it in because it is 11 November, and in my gardener's diary the duties scribbled for that day are "Inspect rhyzomes for rot, dredge pond, drain mower-sump, take lemon tree in".

This fourth injunction has been there since 1993, the year the lemon tree arrived. It arrived in June, the birthday gift of a friend, and it arrived in a big beribboned terracotta pot. It was a sturdy little plant, 3 ft high, a mass of glisteningly healthy leaves and, dangling among them, four little green lemons the size of brazil nuts. There was also a fifth dangling item, a booklet assuring me that if I followed the instructions on citrus husbandry, to include bringing it indoors in early November and taking it out again in late May, it would not only give me many years of wondrous fragrance when it blossomed, but also many years of lemons when it fruited.

So my generous friend and I toasted it in gins and

tonics containing emblematic slivers of lemon, to furnish the tree with a clear idea of where its future duties lay, and I promised him that the next time he stopped by for a snort, the lemon bobbing in his glass would have been fresh plucked. It was a promise I was unable to keep, however, because when he came in August, the four lemons had grown neither bigger nor yellower; although I told him that they unquestionably had. After the third drink, emboldened as one gets, he said that he couldn't be sure, but he thought that one of the lemons had actually grown smaller. I laughed, quite a long laugh actually, and said he was mistaken, I had a ruler, I had measured all of them, they were coming on a treat.

By the time he returned in November, the tree was inside. I had carried it in on the eleventh, a week earlier, and I was now pretty well recovered, except for a slight twinge in the neck whenever I looked to the left. He remarked that the tree had only three lemons on it, was one of them in our drinks, and said yes, and he said, funny, I could swear it's the smallest that's missing, and I said, yes, it had been, but it had suddenly sprung up, rather the way children do, so I had plucked it in his honour, would he like a nut? He ate the nut, a cashew that, poignantly, bore a strong resemblance, in size and consistency, to the fourth lemon; which had, as you will have guessed, fallen off while I was struggling in with the tree. As we sat there, a few leaves also fell off, and he looked at me, but I said it was autumn, they did that, it was in the book.

Which was true. It was also true that the book said the leaves would come back in May, after I had taken it outside again, but only about a dozen did, although the

36

three lemons were still there. Somewhat smaller by now, and greyer than I recalled lemons being, but it was probably just a stage they were going through, I said to my friend at my June birthday party. Whether this was true, neither of us had the chance to discover, because another guest brushed past the tree on his way to get a drink, and the three lemons fell off. When they hit the terrace, they sounded like stones. Are you sure you're following the instructions, said my friend, and I said, to the letter, another week of sun and they'd have been enormous, but look, there's a blossom. And there was; but the next day as I watered it, a bee climbed into the blossom and it fell off.

That was four years ago, since when no blossom at all has appeared, and, of course, no lemons. But, even as you read this, I shall be lugging it in again, because it still has a couple of curly leaves on it. Could be the last time, though. All things considered, I rather think that it shall not grow old as we that are left grow old.

# *A Credit To Oxford*

WHEN, not so very long ago, the credit card slipped into our lives and changed them for ever, it was able to do so by making us one simple promise. It had pondered long and hard about that promise, because it had to be a very good promise indeed if we were to be persuaded that changing our lives for ever was the right thing to do, and the credit card knew that this end could not be achieved by promising us that we should always have something to scrape the ice off our windscreens, or free our molar gaps from raspberry pips, or clear crumbs from our tablecloths or even break into premises by opening locks to which we lacked the key. It knew that it had to reach far deeper into the collective psyche to locate and fondle that subconscious G-spot which would make it irresistible to us.

So the credit card promised that it would say more about us than cash ever could. For it had concluded that what we most wanted the world to say about us was that we had so much money that we didn't need money at all, because an organisation with more money than anybody had such trust in us that it would pick up any tab on our behalf. All we had to do when the tab was presented was lay the card beside it whereupon our creditor would immediately fall to the Axminster and kiss our hems.

After a bit, of course, once that wondrous status had been conferred on so many punters that its wondrousness was inevitably diminished, new wondrousness had to be introduced, first by the gold card then by the platinum, each saying even more about us than cash ever could. It now said that we were not just rich, but so rich that we had to be someone a bit special to have got that rich in the first place.

At which point the credit card suddenly discovered it had run out of precious metals. This was a serious problem: with more and more platinum cards about, more and more rich people wanted even more said about them than mere platinum ever could, but there were no superior ores available to say it. What was the credit card to do?

I'll tell you what it was to do. It was to send me a brochure. It hit my mat this morning. On the cover is a picture of The University of Oxford Visa card. Open the brochure, and inside you will find two dozen pictures of college Visa cards, alongside a smarmy rubric declaring that you can now apply for a Magdalen Visa card, a Balliol card, a Wadham card, and so on. I rang Visa. No, I didn't need to have been at any of these colleges to qualify, all I needed to have was the cash which the card would say more about me than. And since a tiny percentage of each transaction goes to the college, what it patently says is that the bearer is supporting his *alma mater*. He is an Oxford man. Watch waiters fawn! Watch osteopaths goggle! Watch checkout lovelies swoon!

I shall not, of course, be applying for any of these, since for some irritating reason All Souls has not signed up to the scheme, and theirs is the only card I'd want to flash apart from the Rowing Blue Visa card, which, sadly, isn't offered, either. I shall just have to bide my time, until the next inevitable status-hike. It might well bring the Eton Visa card and I shouldn't mind one of those. It would knock their socks off at Cricklewood Donuts. Either that or the Brigade of Guards Visa card, ticketyboo for buying a James Locke bowler, they'd probably chuck in a bespoke baseball cap gratis and bow you to the tinkling door, very nice.

Not, mind, that there isn't one tiny snag to all this, already spotted, I'm sure, by anyone unsettled at the prospect of being spotted; for while it is one thing to plonk down your impressive plastic in Crockfords or

Asprey's or some equally public arena, it is quite another to have it clocked by someone who immediately bellows: "Good God, a Wykehamist, which house, which year, did you have old Ratty ffolkes-Simcox for Greek, too?" or "Stone me, a 2 Para Visa card, we must have been at Goose Green together, come and have a large one!"

For that, I'm afraid, is the inbuilt curse of the credit card's latest quantum leap. It now says more about you than truth ever can.


# *Fag Break*


I CAME out, yesterday. I came out in homage to Oscar Wilde. A bit of a surprise, that, not least to me: it had never been my plan to come out yesterday; Tuesday is the day I stay in and write this, but I could not have written this unless I had first come out – from which you will gather that I have not only come out, but also come back. Why did I suddenly decide to come out? Because I had seen, on Monday evening's news, the unveiling of Maggi Hambling's delightful statue of Oscar, and immediately realised that I would have to come out first thing next morning to make sure my eyes, during that brief television clip, had not deceived me. So, a couple of hours ago, I came out, eyes included, to the fresh-hallowed spot behind Trafalgar Square, and joyfully confirmed that they had not.

Oscar was actually doing it. He was doing it out there, in full public view, at the busy bottom of Adelaide Street. Oscar was engaging in the love that dare not speak its name – not furtively, as I and those like me, a century on, engage in it, not shamefacedly, not mutely begging society's sympathy for a vice impossible to restrain, but flagrantly, relishingly, defiantly. Oscar was smoking. More yet, he was flourishing his cigarette as if it were the most natural thing in the world. And, most yet, he will be doing this for as long as bronze and granite last.

I punched the air. I cried: "Yes!" And I came out. Which is to say I lit up as I never light up, these days, except behind closed doors and in the company of consenting adults – flourishing the pack, snapping the Zippo, sucking deep, exhaling far, yielding, for once, no quarter to the terrified shrieks and fisted threats of the ambient passive, but instead beckoning to the literal outcasts pitifully lurking in the chill huddled doorways of their smoke-free workplaces to come out with me and strut their stuff upon the public street. Tobacco Pride.

A big day for me, then. Did a tear prick the eye, and was it more than windblown ash? You bet. For you who are not as we are cannot possibly imagine how it feels to be set apart, to walk, smoking, into a crowded room and clock the swivelling eyes, sense the dropped temperature, catch the smug tutting and the outraged flare of all those nostrils preening themselves on their self-conferred normality; or how it is to have a host approach, smiling, awkwardly, take your elbow, lead you to a secluded corner and gently but firmly explain that, while he has nothing against smokers personally, while some of his

41

best friends are smokers, while he is a man of the world and knows only too well that it isn't just writers and actors and artists and other bohemian types who are tragically prey to this, er, indulgence, but some of the most eminent people in the land, bishops, bankers, headmasters, general practitioners, Cabinet ministers, members of the Royal Family, even, nevertheless...

I'm not sure, mind, whether rejection by the overtly hostile isn't preferable to the bogus caring of the fascinated prurient: "I hear you're a smoker, I don't think I've ever met one to actually talk to, how did it start, was it some older boy behind the bike shed, did you get into conversation with a man on the common who offered you a cigarette, were you perhaps in the navy, could you ever bring yourself to tell your parents, don't you worry about catching some dreadful disease, I mean some people would say, not me necessarily, that it's a, forgive me, dirty and disgusting practice, wouldn't they, but do you think perhaps, that smoking itself mightn't be a kind of illness, couldn't you be cured if you found the right person, not that I would argue that it was, well, natural, if God had wanted people to smoke, he would have put chimney-pots on our heads wouldn't he, ha ha ha, no offence, I trust..."

So how, you ask, do I respond to all this? I do not respond at all. I just sit there, suffering in my enforced smokelessness, gazing past my interrogator at the window on to that outside world into which I dream of soon escaping, for a fag. You never saw a man who looked with such a wistful eye upon that little tent of blue which smokers call the sky.

# Shop Till You Drop

I STAND, today, in great debt to Dr David Lewis. What about it, you cry, every man in the country stands in great debt to him, he is the brilliant psychologist who last week declared that all men risk instant heart attacks if they try to do any Christmas shopping – just walking past Selfridge's window induces male stress levels normally recorded only when a Tornado pilot spots a missile in his mirror, or a copper finds himself staring down the sawn-off end of something unpredictable. So then, since Dr Lewis has told all the nation's wives that if they don't want to become all the nation's widows they must tuck up all the nation's husbands in front of a roaring fire with a magnum of claret and a pile of ham sandwiches, no crusts, while they themselves rush about accumulating the yuletide gubbins, what makes my debt so special?

What makes it so special is that Dr Lewis has done not only all this for all men, but also, for me, solved a 2,000-year-old riddle. The solution is contained in a sidebar to his report, stating that when men actually steel themselves to do Christmas shopping, they do it, in order to reduce their agitation, at the last minute, buying the first thing they see. Which, at last, sheds all the light we scholars have hitherto sought on the mysterious case of the Three Kings of Orientar and the bizarre gifts they carried with them to Bethlehem.

I realise, of course, that for non-scholars among you the location of Orientar is itself a mystery which has

43

annually nagged at you down the long carolling years, but we dabber hands at exegesis are now firmly convinced that Orientar is a rhyme-enforced abbreviation of Orient'R'Us, a supermarket chain specialising in everything from brass gongs and kaftans to spice racks and hookahs, and very probably – such has been the rigorous nature of our scholarship – cognate with the Aladdin's cave featured in the Christmas panto, which, you'll recall, if it supplies a gift you don't like, for example a lamp, will be happy to exchange it.

Just the sort of portmanteau establishment to appeal to frantic last-minute male shoppers stuck with the problem of gifts for a faraway family of which they knew little. Oh, sure, they would have begun, like us, by coming up with lots of imaginative possibilities: they would have sat down weeks before, with a papyrus pad and a nice sharp quill, and, Caspar having pointed out that Joseph was a carpenter, Melchior and Balthazar would doubtless have agreed that a state-of-the-art toolbox was just the job, or a fabulous multipurpose drill, possibly a folding workbench, jot that down, now what about Mary, lingerie is always a winner, you can't go wrong with a nightie, or perhaps a peignoir, perfect, she'll have the baby by then of course, a wide choice there, romper suits, mobiles, bouncer, pull-along duck…

The list complete, they gird their loins, and pop down to the shops. But lo! there are windows full of 87 different sorts of toolbox and 23 assorted folding workbenches, there are lingerie emporia with 1001 nighties, which material, which colour, what's her size, you go in, no you, why me, what do I know about women's thingies, let's get the baby's present first, blimey, look at that, the place is packed, there must be a million screaming kids in there, I feel dizzy, Caspar, my heart's going like the clappers, Melchior, I have come out in a muck sweat, Balthazar, tell you what, why don't we sit down somewhere, have a drink, two possibly, it is no good rushing these things, we could do ourselves a mischief, we'll just sort ourselves out and come back later when it's not so busy, yes, I'm up for that, me too, call a camel!

So, do they go back? Of course they don't. On the way home, they pass their local branch of Orient'R'Us, oh look, spot on, we can get everything we want here, so in they run. And while they find, of course, no power tools, no nighties, no toys, there is gold, always an acceptable gift, Caspar, and frankincense, can't go wrong with female fragrances, Melchior, and what's that box next to it, the label says myrrh, what's myrrh when it's at home, Balthazar, who cares, what does it matter, he's only a kid.

# *Homo Cricklewood*

I HAVE, this morning a bone to pick. Two bones, as a matter of fact, and it isn't the first time they've been picked, either. The first time was eight years ago when they were more literally picked, by a farmer in the Languedoc. For it was while Jean-Claude Guilhaumon was digging over his little hillside vineyard in 1992 that his *pic* threw them up. The bones were enormous, and thus made Jean-Claude holler in celebration, for the very good reason that he had always dreamt of finding something to stop his dodgy tractor from running downhill and he now spotted that these bones were whatever the French is for just the ticket. That is why they spent the next seven years propping M Guilhaumon's front wheels.

But there are there no longer. As you may have read in your newspaper last week, they have just shot to palae-ontological stardom and been carried off triumphantly to France's Natural History Museum, probably in a white stretch-limo – through whose departing dust the poor old tractor could doubtless be seen rolling haplessly to the bottom of the hill – since the bones have proved to be nothing less than the busted femur of the largest flesh-eating dinosaur ever found in France. Which means that history will now remember M Guilhaumon as something more than a sap with a brakeless tractor, for it was none other than he himself who made the saurian connection: on a visit to a nearby museum last month, Jean-Claude noticed that one exhibit bore a striking resemblance to his ad hoc chocks, and summoned a local old bones whiz, who promptly turned cartwheels; because the two lumps belonged to the abelisaurid family of dinosaurs, previously thought to have been confined to the southern hemisphere.

After which joyful identification, serious stubbly kissing will almost certainly have taken place, followed by major inroads into the Guilhaumon vineyard's better stock though that is, of course, only my guess. I wasn't there.

I was here. Which brings us, as how could it not, to the bone I have to pick with me. Because I sit here in the loft this morning, still racked by the conjoint pangs of guilt and self-pity I have been suffering all week as the consequence of staring down at a garden which, over the past 30 years, has probably yielded enough osseous gubbins to have ensured not only my own immortality after I myself have gone to be a casketed xylophone, but, even more important, the immortality of the village I cherish. For, given the frequent imponderability of the hundreds of misshapen bones I have forked up during those three decades, I may well I have let the hitherto merely legendary Homo Cricklewood slip through my tines, squandered the opportunity to prove the contentious theory that the Diplodocus family had indeed passed this way en route to Willesden from Swiss Cottage, failed to wonder whether the peculiar bits and bobs which get dredged up during my pond's annual clean mightn't have broken off a coelacanth, fallen down in my duty to pinpoint beyond dispute the fabled pterodactyls' graveyard, and cavalierly ignored the possibility that what I found while replanting the rockery in 1986 might have been a Missing Link rather than a Missing Cat. I have done all this by going "Yegh" every time a spade came up with a bit of corpse on it, and chucking the unique detritus of fifty million years, perhaps, on to the bonfire, so that it could be recycled as sprinkled ash to make bigger plants for pests to gobble. It is thus not beyond conjecture that my greenfly have grown fat on Tyrannosaurus Barnet.

When what I should have done, 30 years ago, was buy *The Big Boy's Book of Bones*, to identify the precious shards of heritage that I would painstakingly be laying out – numbered, dated, measured – in the shed. I should have taken snapshots from this angle and that, I should have trudged round museums up and down the land, pocketing pamphlets, jotting notes, buttonholing curators. I should have subscribed to arcane journals, joined specialist societies, put ads in personal columns, stuck up posters, launched websites, walked down Oxford Street between two sandwich boards, even, asking "Do you recognise this bone?" – all that would have been the very least I could have done for posterity.

I have thought long and hard about how to make amends, and there seems to be only one option. When my time comes, I shall be buried under my lawn. Given global warming and the fact that I live on a hill, it is not impossible that in a few million years this could be a vineyard. And, who knows, if its owner happened to have a clapped-out tractor...

# Sellphone

WHEN you hear that today's persiflage is being brought to you by a man in an understatedly elegant Turnbull & Asser shirt cosseted by an immensely comfortable Eckorness swivel chair in front of his truly incomparable Apple Macintosh word processor, sipping a Selfridge cup of stimulating Douwe Egbert Colombian coffee and puffing at a Silk Cut Extra Mild commendably low in tar yet astonishingly rich in flavour, you will instantly twig that he is a man in whose heart there has always been a special place for advertising. So special, indeed that he has deliberately misused the word persiflage for the sole purpose of telling you that the best place to look it up and put him right is the matchless *Concise Oxford English Dictionary*, a snip at £16.99.

Friends, you cannot imagine the joy I took in cobbling that paragraph. How refreshingly different it is from the inconsequential witterings with which I normally pester your attention! How packed to the gunwales with stout concrete stuff, not merely graphic and informative, but invaluable to readers still undecided about what to wear or drink or smoke or sit in or type on – and no less valuable to all the many manufacturers and distributors and retailers and ancillary tradesfolk whose livelihoods require the constant movement of goods, and thus, of course, to the national economy on whose vitality the welfare of each and every one of us depends. Think horseshoe nails, and you will very soon appreciate that the consequence of that first paragraph might well be a hip replacement for poor hobbling Mrs Simpkins of Hull or an extra chemistry teacher for stony-broke Cricklewood Comprehensive. That there might also be a bob or two in it for me, we shall come to later.

Now, I know I speak for all of us when I say that there is not nearly enough advertising about. I cannot be alone in the chagrin which strikes when a batch of jolly commercials all too soon makes way for the rest of some duff programme about vets or cooks; or when, eagerly grabbing my morning newspaper in the hope of a brand-new double-page spread trumpeting a Curry's sale, I find nothing but towering columns of earnest editorial anent Kosovo or Blair; or when, on some hitherto delightful drive, enchanting urban billboards peter out to be replaced by a windscreenful of dreary green stuff and sheep; or when, in the small insomniac hours, Classic FM caringly interrupts a couple of Oistrakhs sawing away at Bach's Double Violin Concerto to lift the soul with an allegro haemorrhoid jingle.

So, then, did you not do joyous cartwheels at Monday's news that a new company called Freedom had got into snuggly bed with BT and other suppliers to provide a service whereby you and I will pay nothing at all for our telephone calls, provided we sign up to allow advertisements to be inserted into them? More cheering yet, many of these commercials will be interactive, empowering us – halfway through listening to our brother-in-law banging on about his alopecia – to order a pizza, join the Territorials, buy a previously cherished forklift truck, nice runner, no rust, or treble-glaze the chic cedarette extension we bought last week during a routine call to our dentist. And won't it, furthermore, make hanging on for half an hour even more fruitful than it is at present? For however much we all enjoy listening to 88 synthesiser choruses of *Volare* counterpointed by 88 captivating reminders that we are being held in a queue, these surely pale beside learning that Marks and Sparks has a new range of exciting spring trousers, kindly state Visa number and inside-leg measurement after the beep.

But, can you believe it, hardly had my joy at Freedom's inspired and much-needed expansion of advertising sunk in, than I suddenly saw that it also pointed the way to even more life-enhancing possibilities: why not introduce snappy commercials into all conversation? For, of course, a fee – albeit slightly smaller than the one for which I plan to invoice all those mentioned in my opening paragraph, which will have been read, with any luck, by a few more people than one would bump into in the pub. What fun, during some ponderous dinner-party natter about nannies or President Saddam Hussein, to pop in a trimly turned commercial extolling, say, mild green Fairy Liquid, thereby earning not merely the warm gratitude of guests who had not hitherto realised that hands that do dishes can be soft as your face, but also a quick couple of quid from Procter & Gamble.

Oh look, I have reached the point where this article needs a pay-off. Well, that makes two of us. So my message today is: Let Freedom Ring!

# Sheep Might Fly

IN the centre of my back garden, some fifty feet from the house, there is a large acacia tree. Could be forty feet high: taller, certainly, than the loft in which I currently sit, staring at it. Now, while I normally sit staring at it because I do not know what to write, today is different; today I am staring at it because I do not know what to do.

Which means that today, I do at least know what to write: I shall write about what I do not know what to do about.

What I do not know what to do about is the animal which is stuck in the branches of the acacia tree. It is has been stuck there for some hours. It is so stuck that it cannot come down of its own accord, and since it is halfway up the acacia tree, it is too high for my accord to be of any help to it. Yes, you are right, in such cases the normal course is to call the fire brigade; but this case is a bit less such than that. I cannot call the fire brigade, because the animal is a sheep. You will reply that this should not faze the fire brigade, we have seen London's Burning, there is no job too great or small for these plucky lads, they would have that sheep down in a trice and I do not disagree. I didn't say the fire brigade couldn't do it. I said I couldn't call them.

Let me lower my stare, in your behalf, to the grassy area below the tree. See, it is not as grassy as it should be. That is because the tree is above it. Every year, as the tree spreads wider the lawn grows balder. But this year I decided to remedy that, which is why my lowered stare can also see that the grassless area, about a hundred square feet, is roped off and criss-crossed with twine to discourage birds from dining on the seed with which, a couple of days ago, I sowed the baldness.

It does not, of course, discourage the birds at all. They are not mugs, birds; they have knocked about a bit, and they have learnt that criss-crossed twine is not unlike a Michelin star, criss-crossed twine says this is a top place to eat, this is gourmet heaven, bring the family, tell your friends. No sooner had I finished criss-crossing and gone inside than a hundred square feet of beaks were tucking in. So I went outside again, waving and shouting, and they flew off and stood on the fence. After an hour or so it got dark, and we all went somewhere else.

That night, Mrs Coren suggested I stick a broom in the middle of the patch and put a hat on it. It worked a treat: it was so much clearer than criss-crossed twine that next morning, the clientele trebled. Birds were diving from ten thousand feet. I had sown Pearl Harbor. So since, after a couple of hours, all the fun had somehow gone out of shouting and waving, I telephoned the garden centre where I had bought the seed. Yes, they said, that is one of the curious things about birds: despite having extremely small brains, they nevertheless have just enough IQ to know that a broom with a hat on is a broom with a hat on. What I needed, they continued, was a scarecrow that moved in the wind, such as balloons. Better yet, said Mrs Coren, as I explained why I was putting my coat on, did I remember that place where we used to get inflatable figures for the children's birthday bashes? It was called The Non-Stop Party Shop, in Sydney Street. I think that they had inflatable cats, said Mrs Coren. Those would be just the thing.

They probably would. There is no way of knowing. Having driven from Cricklewood to Chelsea, I discovered that The Non-Stop Party Shop did not have inflatable cats. They had only one inflatable animal. Can you guess what it was? Of course you can; but can you guess why the box declared it to be The Bonking Sheep? I couldn't guess, either, but when I inflated it, I noticed that it had an orifice. Mrs Coren and I looked at the orifice for a bit, and then Mrs Coren observed that the sheep had blue eyes. She asked me if I had ever seen a sheep with blue eyes before. I told her I didn't think so, but then again, I didn't go to many non-stop parties, these days. Do you think it'll frighten the birds off, she said, and I said I don't know, but it scares the hell out of me.

That was Monday, afternoon, just before I took the sheep out into the garden and tied its front legs to two pegs, leaving its back end free to swing about in the breeze. And, do you know, it was a total success: from 2 pm to nightfall, not a bird went near. But it is Tuesday morning, now, and, as you may just have guessed, the breeze went from strength to strength last night. I don't know what time the gale got up, I know only that it did not get up alone, which is why I have a blue-eyed sheep with an orifice in my acacia tree. Now do you understand why I can't call the fire brigade?

# *Queening It*

SINCE today is HM the Queen's unofficial birthday, I know that you will want me not only to wish her many happy unofficial returns on all our behalfs, but also to take this opportunity to reply to those countless thousands of you who wrote to me regarding the recent Buckingham Palace statement that the Queen was exempt, "by reason of her special position", from the law requiring her subjects to wear a rear seatbelt. Were there, you clamoured to learn, any other special dispensations which Her Majesty alone enjoyed?

The reason that I have not replied earlier is because, not surprisingly, there turned out to be a huge amount of painstaking research involved; but I'm delighted to tell you that I am now, at last, in a position to publish in the national interest what I hope with all my heart is a usefully informative – if by no means comprehensive – list.

When not travelling by car, for example, Her Majesty is uniquely entitled to stand upstairs on buses. Should she spit, however, she is liable to the same fine as anyone else, although she would, of course, be given time to pay. On trains, she is allowed to smoke in the lavatories, but not cigars or pipes. She may also lean out of the window without penalty, except on InterCity routes. On the London Underground, she may not go up a down escalator, or vice versa, but she is allowed to jump over the barrier if she hears her Tube train coming, provided she has a valid ticket for the journey. When flying, she is not permitted to get up before the plane has come to a complete halt, but she does not have to take care when opening the overhead lockers. She is, of course, allowed to lean her bicycle against shop windows.

Sport, as you might expect, is a somewhat more complex juridical area for Her Majesty. When bowling, she is permitted to deliver more than one bouncer per over – except in one-day matches – but she is nevertheless required to observe current ECB dress codes and not wear a headscarf when batting or fielding. She can be given out lbw, but never stumped, and in the unfortunate event of a run out, it is her partner who must surrender his wicket, irrespective of fault. As to football, the Queen is allowed, when playing in goal, to move before a penalty is struck, and would not normally be sent off for bad language, unless violence were involved. In rugger, she does not need to call for a mark or leave the field when bleeding, and in tennis she may abuse her racket as much as she likes. In athletic competition, she is allowed four attempts at the high jump and, when throwing the hammer, to put one foot, but not both, outside the circle. The Queen is also uniquely permitted to carry a spare baton in the 4 x 400 relay, in case she drops one. In snooker, she is permitted to pot the six remaining colours in any order she chooses. Should her opponent go down during a boxing match, Her Majesty is not required to walk to a neutral corner.

She is allowed to busk on her highway, but not in public houses which do not have a music licence. In zoos (with the exception of Whipsnade), Her Majesty is permitted to feed the animals.

When it comes to shopping, the Queen is allowed to go through the checkout marked "6 items or less" with 7 items or more, but no special dispensation applies in regard to taking the trolley from the premises. In Post Offices, staff may not ask her to go to the next counter, and in petrol stations she does not have to switch off the engine while filling up, though she must take the cigarette out of her mouth. She is allowed to bring her dog into foodshops, but if it widdles against anything, she is not exempt from prosecution, provided a notice to that effect is prominently displayed.

Should, however, a notice be prominently displayed

in any public place stating that bill stickers will be prosecuted, Her Majesty may safely ignore this, just as she may with impunity disregard any injunction to leave these premises as she would wish to find them. She is not, mind, exempt from the law in the matter of spraying graffiti, and if told to use the footbath before entering a public swimming pool, she is legally obliged to comply. She is allowed to drop litter only in the royal parks, but may walk on the grass wherever she takes a fancy to do so.

And finally, when driving – in addition to the seatbelt dispensation with which we began all this – Her Majesty is also allowed to hoot after 11 pm, and overtake in the Blackwall Tunnel. If she were to park on a double-yellow line, however, her car would be liable to be towed away, but only by a peer of the realm, with a silken rope.

# Maybe It's Because I'm a Landowner

THIS is a big morning for me. It is as big a morning as I have seen in 40 years, it is a morning that stands poised to change the entire course of my life, because, having spent those four decades searching for a style with a y, I suddenly find myself searching for a stile with an i. Two stiles, in fact – one for my eastern fence, one for my western.

Now, you will say: hang about, that is a bit pretentious even for him, his fences should be called left and right, they are only 50ft apart, you do not need map co-ordinates for a suburban garden, a Cricklewood lawn does not call for a compass, you can distinguish between his herbaceous borders without a sextant, but you are wrong.

Any minute now, people will be tramping down my road with Ordnance Survey Sheet No 176 and they will be serious people, they will have stout boots, they will have sturdy sticks, they will have woolly hats, they will have lumpy knapsacks, and they will be thinking in terms not of left and right but of east and west for that is the kind of serious people they are.

And you may be sure they will not take it at all kindly if, having gone to all the trouble of navigating by the stars and working out my longitude to three decimal points to get to my eastern or my western fence, they then find that they cannot climb over it. They will very likely start kicking it with their stout boots, or banging their sturdy sticks on it, or, at the very least, poking their woolly-hatted heads over it and shouting "Oy!", and that is the last thing I want. Which is why the first thing I want is a pair of stiles, set in my two fences so that serious people can climb over them.

Because, thanks to the generosity of our great Environment Secretary, they will any minute now have the Right To Roam, and it is incumbent upon each and every one of us to be ready for them. Indeed, to welcome them with open arms, for they are paying us a very great compliment in wanting to ramble across our premises: they have waited a long time to see my daffodil fluttering and dancing in the breeze, to have a squint inside my lovely shed, to feel the hoe, sketch the shears, sniff the Paraquat, to take one another's photographs leaning on my rustic Homebase bench, climb to the top of my towering rockery from which it is possible, on a clear day, to see three major roads, and, scrambling down to the shimmering expanse of water beneath, step across it, and find some sheltered spot – beside my sun-dappled car, perhaps, or on my mossy kitchen step – to eat their organic sarnies and brew their herbal tea.

I cannot for the life of me understand why so many of my fellow landowners were so enraged at the announcement of the proposed legislation, so fearful of the imminent incursions of the wandering nerd, so desperate to hurl themselves into the battle to exclude him. For myself, I cannot wait for the first green anorak to clamber over my fence, mistake me for the gardener, and, chucklingly set straight on the matter, whip out his ring-bound notebook and rain-proof pen and begin keenly to quiz me on local lore.

How I long to point out the rutted bit of lawn which stands as undisputed evidence of where the extinct Crickle once flowed, through the boar-packed wood of which my gnarled acacia is the sole survivor! How I yearn to take his arm and lead him to the sacred site, possibly by the dustbins, maybe behind the garage, where rumour has it that woaded Corens fought to the last man to thwart Caesar's march on Hendon! How I relish the thought of filling him in on the restless ghosts of drawn and quartered highwaymen who, having once lurked beside my compost heap to plague the Edgware Stage, now cry "Stand and deliver!" every Martinmas Eve. I may even take them up to the Big House to show them the unique systems of plumbing and pointing and guttering and drive-laying created, just for me, by generations of itinerant artists who brought to Cricklewood the arcane techniques honed to perfection on the bothies of Limerick.

I may start doing cream teas. I may take a correspondence course in morris dancing. I may embark upon the felt-tip monogramming of souvenir items in lustrous Crickleware from *BHS*, or bottling zesty relishes and acne remedies distilled from my own conkers, or stringing chic necklaces of interesting local pebbles, and set up Ye Olde Estate Suitcase, by the gate, to sell them. Aha, you cry, so that is the truth of it, he supports the Right To Roam because he sees a bob or two in it, but you are wrong. I support it because, for those 40 long years, I have been only a mere householder. But today, thanks to Michael Meacher, I am a landowner.


# *Clever Clogs*


THIS ought to be a really snappy piece. It should knock your socks off. That is because I have just walked to the Nautilus Fish Bar and back, and, in consequence, have not only taken my own socks off to write it – the distance being two paved miles and the Cricklewood weather equatorial – but have also improved my mental abilities no end. Now, you will immediately cry: Aha, his mental abilities have improved no end because he has been forking down the Nautilus's peerless cod, cerebral nourishment of kings, his brain cells will be pumping iron, his cortices will be bubbling to the boil, his synapses will be flashing and crackling like Chinese New Year... but you are wrong.

If all that you describe is indeed happening – and I have to say that, so far, it still seems a bit quiet up there – it will have nothing to do with fish. The Nautilus is significant only by virtue of being a mile from my gate, which means that walking there and back takes exactly 45 minutes. Longer, of course, if you stop for cod, but I did not. I stopped for nothing: I walked to the door, waved at the three jolly fryers (if God forbid, the Nautilus is ever taken over by a brewery, at least there might be an apt pub sign to commemorate its heritage) and walked straight home again. For it was only the 45-minute walk that I needed. I needed it because Professor Arthur Kramer, of the University of Illinois, had told me so. Writing in the current *Nature* of his pokings about in the frontal lobes of sexagenarian sluggards, the professor cites proof that if people over 60 walk briskly for 45 minutes, they can, thanks to a five per cent increase in oxygen intake, "significantly improve mental abilities which otherwise decline with age".

I was into my brogues and out the door in seconds. Mine is a trying trade at the best of times, and since this very week marks 40 years of my trying it, who can say with any certainty whether the best of times might not already lie far behind me? I may currently be in the worst of times. My life might have become a Tale of Two Wags. There is no way of measuring, in this game, whether you have lost it, or by how much. It is not like putting the shot. But if walking for 45 minutes can refresh the parts that can do no better than come up with an old advertising cliché to describe what might be going on, it is surely worth a punt.

The snag, however, is that I am back home now, and I do not know if I am any smarter. I have gone back to the crossword clue I couldn't fathom this morning, and it remains unfathomable. Should I do the walk again? Should I do it again after that? I would have to keep choosing different routes, of course, because the three jolly fryers will grow progressively less jolly if I keep approaching their premises only to disappear again. They will conclude that I have gone off their fish.

There is also the risk that, after 135 minutes, I could overdose and wind up too smart: I might get home again and fancy a major career change – particle physics, perhaps, or seriometry, or geodetics, jobs which after only 45 minutes I know so little about that I may have invented one of them, but which, after ten per cent more oxygen, I could easily chuck up this well-paid trade for, especially as my brain has so far deteriorated that I now have two clauses which prepositions are the last word in.

Then again, I'm not sure I can walk briskly for 135 minutes. I am feeling fairly knackered after 45, and may well, as the result have to spend more time than usual sitting down, which might send my mental abilities back to square one. Whatever that means: I think I used to know once; maybe if I got up and walked about briskly, just for a couple of minutes, it would come back to me.

I have tried that, and it hasn't. It might have done, but where I walked briskly to was the bookshelves to look up "square one", but when I got there, I found myself looking up "briskly" instead. I don't know why, it seems to happen more and more after 60, and at least I learnt one new thing; which is that briskly derives from the French *brusque*.

Does this mean that, if Professor Kramer's research were translated into French, his sexagenarian readers would be tempted to spend 45 minutes a day walking brusquely? It would be an entirely different sort of walk. It might not improve their mental abilities at all. It might also lead to unwanted consequences: certainly, if I were to walk brusquely to the Nautilus Fish Bar, turn brusquely on my heel, and brusquely walk away, they might never serve me again. I'll say this for Professor Kramer: he gives you a lot to think about. If you can.

# *Pussy Galore*

Is it any wonder that, when it comes to T S Eliot, pond owners are ambivalent? On the one hand, he spoke for all of them in imperishably declaring April to be the cruellest month: while pond owners do not care one way or the other about breeding lilacs out of a dead land, they worry themselves sick, every April, about breeding frogs out of a dead pond, because April is when frogs descend upon our ponds to breed, and when, as the direct result, the cruellest things happen to them.

Which brings us, unfortunately, to T S Eliot's other hand: for he loved not frogs, but cats, the more practical the better, and, thanks to an irony which must have the old Modernist spinning gleefully in his grave, it is practical cats which are the very source of the April cruelty.

Here's how it works. Of all the many things they like killing, cats like killing frogs best. Frogs are not only less elusive than mice and sparrows, they taste better. We know this because if they didn't, Frenchmen would be called Mice or Sparrows.

However, for 11 months of the year, frogs are elusive enough to escape the feline diet, since, as soon as a paw appears at the edge of their pond, the frogs leap from reed or lily pad and scull rapidly out of harm's way. But they cannot do this in April, because in April frogs have big heavy things on their backs. They have other frogs there. Which, for cats, practical enough to have sussed this out, means *in flagrante delicious*; and, for me, means April days spent heartbrokenly shovelling up the inedible bits of lovers for whom, just as the earth moved, so did the cat.

For 30 springs, I have sought to stop this happening, but there was no way of deterring the cats from the pond. Until this year. This April, I shall know what to do, and I shall know it thanks to none other than the brothers Saatchi, who gave me what I know by knowing more about me than I knew myself. Five weeks ago, their agency phoned me out of the blue and invited me to audition for a TV commercial, God knows why, I am not an actor, I had never done a voice-over before, but I thought why not, so a car came to Cricklewood and took me to Soho, where I was told that Maurice and Charles were breaking the advertising mould with the first-ever Whiskas commercial designed to appeal not to owners, but to cats. Months of research had gone into finding the sort of screen images which attracted feline attention, and all that the resultant film now lacked was a soundtrack designed to do the same. The Saatchis, in short, wanted a man to whom cats would listen. They had auditioned many, to no effect; night after night, the brothers had wept into their pillows, and gnawed their teddies furless. Until, oh joy, the night of 20 January. That night, they slept like tops. They had found their man. They had gone to Cricklewood and come back with Doctor Dolittle.

A week later, the commercials started going out. Friends rang up and said was that you talking to cats just now, and I said yes, put your cat on, ha-ha-ha, all that, but the one uncertainty among all this jollity was, of course, about whether the cats would respond. Would they mark what they had seen and I had said, and begin dragging their owners down to Tesco to strop themselves against the pyramids of Whiskas in purring supplication?

Well, a month has passed, the world has held its breath, and at last, this week, the results are in. M & C Saatchi just rang me. They were beside themselves. They could hardly speak. Research had shown that 8 out of 10 cats had preferred the Whiskas advert: the agency had miles of footage from hundreds of cameras focused on thousands of cats who had lain yawning on rug and sofa, absently licking this and that while countless other adverts jostled on their fireside screens, but had suddenly sprung up, ears pricked, eyes rolling, saliva spouting, when a voice murmured into the room, speaking fluent Cat.

You will cry, lucky devil, his options are endless, he is sitting on a goldmine, he could stick up a brass plate saying Cat Interpreter, No Job Too Large Or Small, All Credit Cards Accepted, he could be the millionaire star of *One Man And His Cat*, with a couple of keen tabbies he could break the record for sheep in a phone booth, never mind pantomime, this man could train a cat to do anything, punters would cross oceans to watch the pas-de-deux from *Dick Whittington* – but I have my sights on none of these. I want to make only a tape-recording which will spend April running continuously beside my pond, warning: "These frogs are being genetically modified." That should keep the cats off. Well, 8 out of 10, anyway.

# *Ah, Yes, I Remember It Well!*

WE had been watching happily for the best part of a bottle when my wife said: "Oh, blast, I think a dog's going to come round the corner in a minute."

In a minute, a dog came round the corner.

"Well, that's it, then," she said. "We've seen it before."

"I thought we might have done," I said, "half an hour ago. When they pulled the body out of the water with the boathook."

"Why didn't you say anything?" she said.

"I wasn't sure," I said. "They're always pulling bodies out of the water with boathooks. I might have been remembering an old *Morse*, or an old *Wexford*, or an old *Bergerac*."

"Or an old *Taggart*."

"Or an old *Taggart*," I said. "Exactly."

"Instead of an old *Frost*," she said.

I looked back at the old *Frost*. "We could carry on watching," I said. "After all, it's only a boathook and a dog, we don't know how it ends. We don't know who dunnit."

"We might remember," she said. "There's another hour to go. We might suddenly remember after 45 minutes. I think there's a bit, later on, where he argues with his Superintendent. It might jog our memory. It might all come back."

"They all argue with their Superintendents," I said. "It didn't jog our memory in that *Midsomer Murders* we watched last week."

"No, it didn't," she said. "What jogged our memories in that was the nurse on the bicycle."

"It didn't jog mine," I said. "I was enjoying it. You could've kept quiet about it. You could've just carried on watching."

"No, I couldn't. As soon as I saw the nurse on the bike, I remembered, and then I remembered there were two slit throats coming up, and then I remembered the killer was the twerp in the blazer. I couldn't have just sat there after that could I?"

"He was only pretending to be a twerp," I said.

She looked at me.

"Hang on," she said, "if you remembered as well, what was the point in either of us watching?"

"I didn't remember then," I said. "I've only just remembered now."

"You might have remembered then," she said. "We might have both carried on watching, with just me knowing we'd seen it after the bike bit, until something else happened half an hour later which jogged your memory, and I'd have been watching for half an hour for nothing."

"It's called marriage," I said. "It is fraught with that kind of thing. I might have not had my memory jogged at all, and then at least one of us would've been happy."

"Happy," she said, "is putting it a bit strong. I didn't even think much of this one..." she waved her glass at the screen "...when we saw it the first time."

"You didn't say that while we were watching it this time," I said, "for the hour before the dog came round the corner."

"It wasn't the hour I didn't think much of the first time," she said. "Now I know it was the one with the dog, I can remember not thinking much of the whole thing, after it had finished the first time."

I reached for the remote, and switched off. "Don't you want to know who dunnit?" she said.

"Not enough to sit through it for 45 minutes – until he has the row with his Superintendent," I said. "Even if it doesn't jog my memory, it might jog yours, and I wouldn't want to carry on sitting through it knowing you knew who dunnit and just weren't saying."

"But we're not even certain this is the one where he's going to have the row," she said. "It might be the one where his dim but lovable sergeant asks for a transfer to traffic division because his wife is pregnant again and wants him back home at a reasonable hour. If it is that one, the car blows up."

"No, I remember the one where the car blows up, and it didn't have a boathook or a dog that came round the corner. Anyway, it wasn't his car. Frost's car has never blown up. You're thinking of Dalgleish's car."

"The Triumph roadster with the dickie seat?"

"No," I said. "That is Bergerac's car."

"There's one *Morse* we've seen three times," she said. "It was cars that reminded me. Morse's nice old red Jag got dented. You winced."

"I could only have winced the first time," I said. "I wouldn't have forgotten a thing like that."

"Who are you kidding?" she said.

I picked up the programme guide, and peered at it. "God, I hate the summer," I said, after a bit. "Would we have seen *Have I Got Old News For You*, with Eddie Izzard? Before it had the Old in it, I mean?"

"Is there anything left in that bottle?' she said.

# Stone Me

FORGIVE me, but for over an hour now I have been lying here on my attic couch as oft I do, in vacant or in pensive mood, and I'm afraid I have no option but to share with you what, during all that time, has been flashing upon my inward eye. I have to share it with someone or go crazy, and there is nobody else around. From which you may gather that it is not daffodils which are flashing upon my inward eye, but something far less blissful: what my inward eye has flashing upon it is Cary Grant. Cary Grant is standing on my lower lip and he is trying to push Eva Marie Saint up my nose. Not, let me quickly say, up the inside of my nose – if that was what my inward eye had to handle, I should already have gone crazy – but up the outside. They are trying to get to the top of my head. It is taking them ages.

Now, you who have all seen *North by Northwest* will be muttering to yourselves: "What is he banging on about; there is no way that Cary and Eva could be climbing his face, he is not Washington or Jefferson or Lincoln or Roosevelt, he is not part of Mount Rushmore at all, he is part of Cricklewood? Cary and Eva would never climb to the top of anything in Cricklewood", to which I would reply: "All that you mutter is true, but it is nevertheless on the cards that the four big stone Presidents you mention could easily end up in Cricklewood, and if they did, my head would be beside theirs."

The cards which this is on arrived this very morning, forwarded by my American publisher, to whose address they had been sent from Kansas City, by a company called Millennium Memorabilia Inc. If I fill in one of these cards appropriately, enclose three recent photographs of my head – front, back, profile – and enclose an even more recent cheque, or my credit card details, I could, if I allowed 28 days for processing and delivery, end up with a handsome simulated-granite reproduction of Mount Rushmore to grace my den, which would include me. It would, moreover, include me anywhere I wanted to be included: I could be at one end, next to George, or at the other end, next to Abe, or I could be in the middle, between Tom and Teddy. Even moreover, if I chose to spend not $500 but $5,000, and allowed three months for delivery, I could be part of an outdoor version, heads 6ft high, to grace my backyard or pooldeck and impress my neighbours, especially when floodlit. How much my backyard would be graced by five huge heads staring at the house from beside the ailing pond that is the closest thing I have to a pooldeck, I cannot say, but I am on surer ground when it comes to impressing the neighbours: there are a fair number of elderly residents around here who look out of their windows a lot, and any of them getting up for a nocturnal widdle and suddenly spotting the floodlit five gazing fixedly at them from the blanketweed, like creatures from the Black Lagoon, could well be impressed straight into intensive care.

Forget Mount Rushmore then, and thank you so much for helping me to, it's amazing what a little chat with friends can do, I can feel Cary's footprint fading from my lip, I shall be ticketyboo soon. Unless, that is, my back starts playing me up: it's not easy, raising a flag over Iwo Jima, once you have coughed up 500 bucks to be drafted into the

Marine Corps, albeit at several feet below the regulation height, in order to, in the eye-pricking words of MM Inc, "partake in an ikonic moment of American glory". A moment which, I note, does not come in backyard size, probably because you would need a hill to do it justice, exposing it to Japanese tourists passing through who might spot it from their bus and take it so amiss as to come back on 7 December and bomb it. For nationalism is a strange fruit – ask any greengrocer – and if the object is to attract punters "desirous to position themselves among the millennium's most famed Americans", a modicum of sensitivity is advisable, these days. Is MM Inc wise to offer a share in Custer's Last Stand? Apart from the snag of providing three snapshots of an absent scalp, who would wish to be seen dead alongside America's beastliest brute? Nor, remembering Joe Louis on the scrapheap, would any decent US citizen, I hope, wish to grace his den with "a two-foot-square ring, showing you landing a right hook on the Brown Bomber's jaw".

I could, mind, make out a case, even a cheque, for a cobbled duo of Marilyn Monroe standing over a grating and me standing beside her. I think, since you and I seem to have concluded today's business, I might just run that past the inward eye.

# Royal Lowness

As I anticipated even while I still sat semi-glued to Saturday's jolly Wessex nuptials with their neo-traditionalist hotchpotchery of pomp and knees-up, thousands of your e-mails hit my Sunday screen, begging for expert guidance as to how this challenging new cobbling of the royal and the common is to be sustained during what we all pray are the blissful years ahead. I have in consequence spent a couple of hectic days going into all the points your caring correspondence raised, but since I cannot answer each of you personally, let me target today's column upon a typical smattering.

Many of you wanted to know whether the Wessexes would use Tesco's, and, if so, would protocol require the Earl, being royally born, to wait in the car reading the *Sun*, leaving his genetically common Countess to lug the boxes out herself, or would he go in and personally examine sell-by dates, squeeze plums, and so on.

This poser is trickier than it appears. Traditionally, royals try to keep well away from supermarkets because of having to walk round slowly with their hands behind them, asking passionate questions about numbers of chops sold, the secret of stacking bean tins, and how on earth they manage to find fish with fingers. Since, however, this is to be a perfectly ordinary marriage, you are correct in assuming that the couple will indeed be doing their own shopping.

Certain steps, though, have been taken to embrace this innovation within acceptable protocols. A State Trolley has been commissioned, narrow enough to pass down supermarket aisles and pulled by four Shetland geldings selected for their continence by the Comptroller of Gastrology to the Royal Mews. This will be driven by the Earl, while his radiant consort stands on the rear banquette, flicking items off the shelves with the Mace of the D'Urbervilles, a handsome wedding gift from Asprey's incorporating the Chandragore Emerald in its orvidium, now that the curse upon it has been formally exorcised by the Bishop of Norwich.

On a more personal note, Kylie Packenham writes: "I am fascinated by royal precedent, and what I want to know is if the Wessexes decided to go to the pictures only he had other things on first, eg chiropodist, Trooping of Colour, having the cat seen to, and they had to meet at the Odeon, would she have to hang about outside, never mind him being the late one, just because he was the Queen's son, or would she buy the tickets with her own money and wait inside, or would she go in and save the seat next to her and tell the usherette to show him where she was sitting when he eventually turned up?"

Generally speaking, Kylie, this situation is covered by the Consort Entitlement Statute of 1485 when, following the Battle of Bosworth, Anne, wife to Richard III, was allowed by the Lord Chancellor to start dinner without her husband on the grounds that his head was on a stick in the next county. Since then, royal spouses have been permitted to depart from precedent if the circumstances are fittingly extenuating. It is, though, doubtful whether standing outside the Odeon falls into that category. Therefore, the Wessexes will instruct the Master of the Queen's Local Papers to inform them in writing as to the exact time of the film's beginning, he having been formally apprised of their desire not to sit through all the adverts and other rubbish, and a Moving Picture Equerry (or, in Scotland, a Fleapit Ensign of the Queen's Troop) will be charged with ensuring that both royals arrive at the box office simultaneously, where a Ticket Major of the Household Cavalry will be waiting with two best stalls. Should the Countess unavoidably arrive first, she will be invited by the manager to inspect the commissionaire, and given a box of Maltesers to eat while awaiting the Earl.

Which brings me to Mr George Ferris, who asks: "Will they do their own milk order of an evening, and do they have one of them titchy crate efforts or will they just put the empties on the step like normal people? Also, which of them will take the bins out?"

The answer is that empties are traditionally put out nightly by Bottle Poursuivant, though members of the Royal Family usually write their own notes, except in cases of grave illiteracy. The Wessexes, however, intend to take out their own crate, different from the standard model only in being made of tit-repellent gold, affixed to their doorscraper by the Chain of Scone, and guarded by a platoon of Cameron Highlanders. They will not, though, take out their own rubbish. This will be dealt with by the Gentleman Usher of the Black Bag.

# *There Once Was a Hungry Gosling*

I WAS mortified to read, a day or so back, that Miss Germaine Greer had been clobbered by a two-week driving ban and a £540 fine for whizzing through nocturnal Essex at 101mph. What mortified me was not the penalty itself, severe though it was, but the fact that the wondrous narrative fashioned to mitigate the offence had achieved absolutely nothing except the revelation that within the ears of magistrates lies the stoniest ground there is.

For what Miss Greer's lawyer, Kendal Travis, told the Harlow court was that his client had wellied her throttle only because she feared for the lives of her tiny goslings in distant Saffron Walden – who, as dusk fell, had found themselves all alone in a darkling orchard lit only by the eyes of prowling foxes. And as if it were not enough to have a storyteller called Kendal Travis, a setting called Saffron Walden, and a cast of farmyard innocents and villains so traditionally comprised as to have not merely Aesop but Hans Andersen and both Grimms spinning in their graves at the unacknowledged debt, the tale is richer yet. The reason Saffron Walden was distant that night was because Miss Greer was stranded at a glittering party aboard a pleasure steamer in the Thames, racked by fears that if she did not get home by the appointed hour, dreadful things would happen – though whether her Mercedes would have turned back into four mice and a pumpkin, Kendal did not say.

But what he did say should have been more than enough, you would think, to melt the heart of the flintiest beak: here is Miss Greer, admittedly once an icon of turbulence but now a distinguished elderly rural academic, given to tramping her sylvan acres in granny glasses, a fetchingly battered big straw hat, and long flowing chintz, not merely broadcasting gosling fodder from her Prada trug but, as you have read, dispensing love and succour to all creatures great and small; provided, of course, they are dumb, since she has long ago and very publicly, exchanged the hurly-burly of the *chaise-longue* for the deep peace of the single bed. Could there be anyone likelier than this dear little caring spinster to so commend herself to a country magistrate that hardly has the charge been read than his gold pince nez have been whipped off, his Paisley handkerchief has been pressed to his piping eye, and his voice is tremblingly dismissing that charge forthwith and sending the chargee back to her chooks and porkers without a stain on her character?

Manifestly, there could. While I have no way of knowing the reason for the bench's brutal dismissal of Mother Goose's heartrending explanation, I am tempted to guess that he treated the whole thing as just another, well, fairy story. And that – as, knowing me by now, you yourself will have guessed – is the aspect which mortifies me most of all. For I, down the long arches of the years, have put my boot to the floor on many occasions, been sometimes caught bang to rights, and, like all honest motorists, entered a not guilty plea backed by plausible farragos about expiring aunts and unattended infants and gases left on and desperate bladders and three-line whips on this and that. Astonishingly, these never passed muster, yet I continued to live in hope: I should doubtless speed again, be apprehended again, but this time I would a tale unfold whose lightest word would harrow up the JP's soul, freeze his old blood, make his two eyes, like stars, start from their spheres, his knotted and combined locks to part and . . .

It is a hope I can no longer entertain. If the law refuses to concern itself with the distressing trifles of Germaine's pastoral fable, it will assuredly have scant truck with any Cricklewood gallimaufry I cobble together. Sad that I shall never be able, now, to use a terrific story about having to dash back to my pond because the frog had just spawned and there were predatory newts about, but I am off to bin my checked cap and my stringback gloves and chop in my nippy red German ragtop for a sluggish brown Polish estate to keep me on the straight and narrow and egregiously legal. Not for the first time, Miss Greer has compelled men to reconsider their wicked ways.

## Selling It Like It Is

PEER through the peephole. See that hollow-eyed wreck in the corner of the attic? He is the Prisoner of Cricklewood. He is in Cricklewood for life. He has been banged up by Nick Raynsford's imminent Bill requiring all vendors to give all prospective buyers a seller's pack telling the absolute truth about the house they wish to unload.

Such as the fact that it is in Cricklewood. When I bought mine 30 years ago, I believed it was in Hampstead because I had told the agent I was looking for a house in Hampstead, and he said have I got the house for you, meet me at Hampstead Tube, so I did, and we drove to this house, and I bought it, and a week later I walked round the corner of the road he had driven me into, and there was this big sign saying Cricklewood. To estate agents, Cricklewood does not exist – it is Outer Hampstead, or Hampstead borders, or Hampstead-on-the-Wold for that is the only way to flog houses in Cricklewood.

But now, if I want to sell, I shall have to identify it on page one of my seller's pack. Who will get to page two? And if anyone does, what then? He will read about the clunk in the night. The house has gone clunk in the night for 30 years, we have had top men in, it is not the pipes, it is not the boiler, it is not the joists, the clunk is undiagnosable and thus untreatable, the house just waits for night to fall and starts going clunk. Unlike the loft. The loft goes creak all day. I know, because I work up here. It is like working aboard the *Cutty Sark*. We have had top men in, they ask me if it goes creak at night and I say I'm not sure, you can't hear for the clunk, and all that the top men will say is that houses expand and contract and some of them make noises doing it. I shall have to put that in my seller's pack, and the prospective punters who get to page two will wonder if the house will one day either burst or shrivel. Who would go on to page three?

If any plucky soul did, he would only learn about the sashes. This house has three dozen sash windows, several of which can suddenly descend and decapitate anyone mug enough to look out of them. We, of course, do not even look out of the ones which do not suddenly descend, because, if anyone gets to page four, he will find what else can suddenly descend, called roofing tiles, some of which still surround, see page five, the Leaning Chimney of Cricklewood. If the chimney ever suddenly descended, it would mean the end of the terrace, so in all honesty – which Nick Raynsford now requires – this house should be described as "Detached, Possibly End of Terrace".

The house, mind, does boast a wealth of doors, 21 to be exact, though I shall not, sadly, be able to include that sentence when describing them on page six, if I want to avoid swingeing fines for dissembling, since *boast, wealth,* and *exact* do not, like the doors themselves, really fit. Even if I wrote, "21 doors which open and shut", I would be pushing it, unless I added "though not always at the same time", because pushing it is precisely what is required of each of them, at night, when the house has contracted. Some rooms cannot be got out of after midnight. During the day, however, once the house has expanded, several of the doors often swing open of their own accord, thanks to a sudden gust roaring in through a gaping sash some uncircumspect visitor has just missed being decapitated by.

The good side is that most of these doors do not swing fully open, this being one of the benefits of what economical truth describes, on page seven, as "a differentially even flooring system".

Outside? Gloriously south-facing but for a slight

deviation of 180 degrees, there is a broad, emerald lawn in summer and, in winter broad khaki marshland which has attracted top men from all over: regular readers will know, of course, that I have a small pond, but only those who may one day turn to page eight will discover that it can also miraculously transform itself into a large lake at the drop of a shower.

Not, thanks to Nick Raynsford, that there will ever be a page eight, or any other page. Be serious. This is Cricklewood. *Caveat vendor*.

# *After You've Gone*

SINCE we last met, something has been bothering me no end. It is my end. And it is bothering me because I have received a piece of junk mail about what happens to my junk after I am myself junk. It was sent by an outfit which hucksters DIY wills. It wants me to make one.

Hitherto, inheritance has never figured in my life. Last words have yielded me nothing. I have never had an expiring hand draw my ear down to a lip trembling to whisper that the George III cross-banded mahogany breakfront chiffonier which I had long cherished would indeed – and any minute now – pass to me. I have never slit a posthumous envelope to have a little gilt key fall out so that its parent safe-deposit box could cough up a

Patek Philipe gold half-hunter or the green eye of a little yellow god. No discreet legal murmur has ever stayed my hurrying from the graveside with a request to join a gathering in King's Bench Walk for a small brown sherry and the opportunity to dip my bread in the dear departed's gravy. No executor's small ad has ever dangled the tasty off-chance that I might learn something to my advantage.

And lucky is what I count myself. Descent from a long lineage devoid of both money and taste has ensured that the stuff I walk on, and the stuff that stands upon it, and the stuff that hangs on the walls above, is only decor. It is not memory. It is not responsibility. It is not family. I do not have chairs which depress me with the thought of the dead ancestral bums that sapped their springs. My shelves do not bow beneath the weight of half-moroccoed rubbish I shall never read. No rosewood spinet nestles, inviolate, in my chimney corner, smugly confronting me with my inability to play it. And all my clocks tell the right time, because it doesn't take two old crooks in baize aprons and a bill for 600 quid to get them going.

When my ancestors chucked in their sponges, vans came and cleared their premises, and descendants gasped relief. Faded moquette suites were not for bequeathing, nor were Ferguson radiograms, threadbare Axminsters or mural ducks. Bereft kin did not dry their eyes and begin haggling over nests of oakette tables, oleographs of Love Locked Out, or tea sets with flaking transfers of Blackpool Tower still, here and there, adhering to them.

And I thank God for it. Not only because it means I've not been stuck with a debt to the dead – my rooms do not have to live up to the sumptuous presence of this grandpa's bureau bookcase, or that aunt's vast and melancholy study of carthorses approaching Utrecht – but because I owe no hostages to living fortunes, either: I do not have to entertain embittered bloodstock rivals who will sit glowering at the priceless jade collection they always dreamt of inheriting instead of the long-case clock they did, which chimes 36 at 4 am and whose regiments of vintage woodworm have now migrated to their joists. Nor was I ever trapped into that grim blackmail whereby time must be spent with people you don't like in the greedy hope of some day getting your hands on the bits and bobs you do: I could always take or leave my relatives, because I never needed to think twice about whether they were going to leave anything I might want to take. For an heirloom is exactly what its etymology says it is: it is a device for interweaving generations, willy-nilly.

Which now, equally willy-nilly, presents me with a different problem. Because, having successfully avoided incurring any debts to the past, I am stuck with a debt to the future. I have, over the years bought some stuff: it is neither very rare nor very valuable stuff, but it is nice stuff, and, because I like having it around, it will stay here until that day when someone pushes his way through it, puts his stethoscope to my supine chest, and declares that I and the stuff have come to a parting of the ways. I shall be carried out; but the stuff will remain behind. Whereupon – after what I can only trust will be a decent interval – my nearest and dearest will file in and eyeball the stuff, for it will be their stuff, now. A life which avoided heirlooms will have been concluded by a death which manufactured them, and not only will my heirs become unsettled, but my ghost, too. Dispersed, the items which embodied my taste and judgement will reappear in unknown rooms, hapless prey to unguessable responses: valuers will sneer and chortle, beneficiaries moan and wrangle, while I – sealed up and tucked away in the only piece of furniture they let you take – will just have to lie there and bear the whips and scorns of time. All very disquieting.

Dying I can live with. It's my immortal remains that worry me.

# Flower Power

IN all the teeming annals of Clacton-on-Sea, pearl of the Essex Riviera, there can, surely, be no story more resonant than this. It begins in late 1942, when an Afrika Korps sergeant, lately plucked from the Western Desert and relocated to a PoW camp outside Clacton, is set to work on the lush, sloping lawns of the Esplanade Gardens, an exemplary stretch of those broad sunlit uplands which his master intended him to charge up behind a tank, but which he now trudges up behind a lawnmower.

Not that he admires his master. He despises him. He insists he is not a Nazi, and more yet, that he loves

England, and Clacton most of all. Not merely an assiduous gardener but also a civic boon – he dispenses free cuttings, he helps old ladies across roads, he teaches ping-pong in the youth club, he babysits, he sings in the church choir – he so endears himself to Clactonians that, at the end of hostilities, they give him a big farewell party and a bracket clock, inscribed with affection. He wipes away a hot tear, and returns to the Fatherland, in December 1945.

And in March 1946, the hundreds of little crocuses he planted on the Esplanade slopes the previous winter come up through the emerald lawn. In letters 10 ft high, they spell "Heil Hitler!"

I relate this incident now not just because it is part of our common history, but also because it is part of my uncommon autobiography. I was there, in Clacton, in 1946, and though my autobiography has moved on a bit, I am there again now, if only in memory. For I am actually in Cricklewood this morning, staring at my own lawn and giving much thought to the two plump sacks of crocus lying beside me, waiting for the dibber in my left hand to do its job. It cannot, however, do its job until it is shifted to my right hand, and that hand is holding something already. It is holding my clipboard with the lawn plan on it. I cannot start dibbling until I have decided on what to spell out.

I have never needed to crocus a message before. For nearly 30 years, the crocuses I planted when we first moved in not only came forth but multiplied. In 1998, we ended up with hundreds. In 1999, however, we ended up with three; what we had in hundreds was little holes. I didn't spot the holes earlier because the grass is long in winter, which is why I also didn't spot the squirrel eating. I didn't know that squirrels ate crocus – they never had before. Which is why, this autumn, I have to put 300 new bulbs in.

It was only while I was driving back from the nursery that planting a message occurred to me. It did that because I was half-listening to a gardening programme suggesting ways of florally commemorating the millennium, and I suddenly remembered the PoW, and I thought: I shall crocus MILLENNIUM 2000 into the lawn. Naff, you wince? Of course it's naff. Is naffery not the very quintessence of the shenanigans? It would be like having my own Greenwich carbuncle, my own London Eye, my own Sir Cliff Richard standing on my lawn and yodelling the Lord's Prayer to the tune of *Auld Lang Syne*.

But, just as I was jotting a really naff design on my clipboard, a jumbo flew over, low, as many do, and it suddenly struck me that I could kill two birds with 300 crocuses: I could not only dibble a message even naffer than MILLENNIUM 2000. I could fulfil my dream of commending this unknown parish to a wider world. Japs and Belgians, Yanks and Poles, would, as they fastened their seat-belts for Heathrow, binocular down as tourists do, and spot below them the legend: CRICKLEWOOD 2000. I should have put Cricklewood, quite literally, on the map. They would wonder; they would inquire; they would learn. They would *know*.

So that is what I have now done. Or rather, that is what I hope I have now done I should hate all this hard work to end with disembarking foreigners asking "What is ICKLE?" "Who is LEW 20?" or "Where is OD?" I can only pray the squirrels don't get hungry, this winter.

# Perdu For Good

LET'S go, children of the country, the day of glory has arrived! Yes, you are not wrong, I am singing the *Cricklewoodaise*, and you know why, too.

You know that it is our turn, now, for a French revolution, and that, even as you yodel along to my stirring anthem, millions of our countrymen are storming the checkouts of the mighty, baying their rage at all items Froggie and threatening that if these are not immediately dragged from their shelves and defenestrated, heads will roll. To save his own, even our agrominister Nick Brown is venting his private aggro by boycotting Gallic goodies: no more Camembert or Meursault in Nick's house, no more boules in his garden, or Ambre Solaire on his holidaying conk.

Well, we must all make our protests in our own way, and while I accept that my loyal readership will be much reduced this morning – for they are equally loyal to British beef and will be too busy torching their Peugeots, shredding their Dior frocks, and chucking their Le Creuset casseroles at their priceless Limoges collections to open their newspaper – I can only hope that when the long day's ethnic cleansing is done, they will settle down with *The Times* and a large Welsh brandy and discover what I myself am doing for the cause.

I did, of course, think long and hard about giving up burgundy and pâté de foie gras and binning my Pierre Cardin tuxedo, but there are plenty of citizens around who will be doing that and I wanted to make a really major protest which might well be diminished if I were to boycott a lot of other French stuff. More yet, I wanted the protest to be not so much economic as spiritual, by piercing the very heart of that culture of which our enemy is so egregiously proud.

So I have decided to give up Marcel Proust. As soon as I have finished jotting this public statement, I shall take from the shelves the score of precious volumes which comprise not only the two English translations but also the glorious original, and drive them down to Oxfam. It will be a terrible wrench, God knows, but He also knows a thing or two about sacrifice, and that is what protest requires, if it is to mean anything.

Proust and I go back a long way. We've been together now for 40 years: he is my dear old French. In one edition or another, I have not only kept *A la Recherche du Temps Perdu* within virtually instant reach in all the flats and houses I have ever lived in, I have also taken it all over the world, on business trip and holiday alike, and, when I was confined some years ago to a long convalescence, it was beside my bed throughout. Our life together started when I bought the seven-volume Scott Moncrieff version in my first term at Oxford, and hardly a day went by during the subsequent four years that I didn't read it. By the time I came down, I was well past page 50. Page 53, in fact: I can be so certain because when I examine that first volume now, I can see not only the thumbprints and the beerstains and the squashed flies and the cigarette burns of my distant youth, but also that they stop at page 54.

I cannot recall why I read those opening pages over and over again, but no further, and can only assume that it was such a terrific novel that I wanted to savour it slowly, but that I kept getting interrupted.

That I never got beyond page 53 over the subsequent four decades is probably because – in 1967, and in Paris, I see from the flyleaf – I bought the French edition. A bit irritating, since it came with uncut pages, and, though I can't now remember precisely, I feel sure that the fact that only the first 26 pages of the four thousand have been cut must mean that I lost my paper-knife. Either that, or I must have been about to cut the next 3,974 when Terence Kilmartin published his new translation – in 1981, I note from the Hatchard's bill bookmarking between pp 36 and 37 – and I rushed out to buy it.

My eyes fill now, not just at the remembrance of things past, but at the acceptance of things that will never be. Thanks to the literally beastly intransigence of his descendants, my lifelong communion with Proust is at an end. It is time to bung him in the boot for Queen and country, stiffen the lip, and do my plucky best to console myself with a cup of char and a British biscuit. Dunked, of course.

# Vita Longa, Ars Brevis

HAD you, last Saturday afternoon, been a member of the frenzied mob on the Tate Gallery steps jostling towards the revolving doors to get into one or other of their current shows, you might have been startled to see someone suddenly burst, spinning, out of those doors, and not only, like Charlie Chaplin, continuing to spin, but when he had finished spinning, punching the air and shouting aloud.

What energy, you might have thought; but what you should have thought was: what synergy! For I had just seen not one or other of their current shows, but both. I had seen the Art of Bloomsbury and the Turner Prize Exhibition, and if there is a better word for what resulted than synergy, I do not know it.

I know only that as I stood before the work of, first, those for whom art was everything, and, next, those for whom everything was art, my heart leapt at what the conflation implied. I suddenly realised that there was a set of aesthetes both mutually influential, like the Bloomsberries, and also dab hands, like the Turnerees, at cobbling art from mundanity. It was, of course, the Cricklewood Group.

Take my neighbour three doors up. Let us call her Vanessa Emin. Her *Parallel Arrangement of Wheelie Bins* has changed the way the traditionalists among us have always treated this compelling subject, mainly as the result of the stirring manifesto she shoved through eyeryone's letterbox. Up until then, my own *Wheelie Bin*

*With Lid Up and Stuff Poking Out* was something of which I had been quite proud, though it admittedly lacked the panache of Damien Beerbohm opposite in his *Wheelie Bin With Lost Lid and Windblown Rubbish All Round It*, or the radical work of Duncan McQueen, the Group's persistent rebel, in his *Bugger Bins, Give Me Plastic Bags Any Time*, which attracted much attention, particularly from cats and foxes. However, Vanessa's fresh approach and the passion with which she advanced it were not to be denied. The whole Group works with two shut bins, now.

Argument, of course, is the lifeblood of any aesthetic movement. When Lytton Wilson, one recent Sunday, began his controversial work *Strimming At Dawn*, many members of the Group ran into the street in their nightclothes to express their views so forcefully that blows might well have been exchanged, had their attention not been diverted by John Maynard Peppin, the installationist on the corner engaged in his major opus *Putting In A New Bathroom*, who had discovered that the cheapest time to have a skip delivered was before 1 am. As a result, the other members of the Group, confused now as to which new piece was more deserving of their critical attention, returned to their own studios, but – such is the serendipity of conceptual art – not before creating an entirely original atonal masterpiece, *Concerto for Slamming Doors*.

As for our own experiments in the video art which comprises three-quarters of the Turner output, how much further the Cricklewood Group has, by working together, advanced this vibrant genre. Transfixed by the three hours spent next door watching Dora and Roger's

*People With No Heads Running About On the Costa Brava*, I immediately borrowed their camcorder, which enabled me to shoot my seminal trilogy, *Tillie's Wedding With Thumb, Lord's Test Match On Diagonal Pitch With Thumb,* and the minimalist finale, *Thumb.*

At its premiere, John Maynard Peppin was so inspired by this that, after he woke up, he borrowed the camera to make his *Man Rummaging About In My Skip*, with its dramatic ending in which a ball-cock flies towards the lens. The film, sadly, attracted much adverse comment, both from the copper who felt that its debt to Dora and Roger's technique of not filming heads constituted a waste of police time, and from Dora and Roger, whose insurers failed to cough up on the ground that the camcorder was being used by somebody else.

But, then, the Cricklewoodies have always governed their lives by the proposition that all art is a fusion of agony and ecstasy. Even if we can't recall who said it. Michelangelo? Tracey Emin? Someone of that calibre, anyway.

# Pillow Talk

Last Friday, as the joyous huzzahs echoed across the length and breadth of our own dear queendom and the wondrous news beaconed from channel to channel and complete strangers hugged one another in every street while the welkin above them filled with flying hats, even the ranks of Tuscany could scarce forbear to cheer.

Especially the ranks of Tuscany, in fact, because hardly had the thrilling story broken before the entire Italian population sprang excitedly to their pocket calculators and, with all that wily meticulousness which the Vatican has made second nature to them when it comes to the timing of their first nature, worked out that the new Blairling must have been conceived during its parents' August vacation. What Cherie was going to have was a bambino.

But, next day, the Tuscan cheering became a broken sob. For what Cherie was actually going to have was a little cheri(e). As Melissa Kite reported in *The Times*: "A rose-brick château in the South of France is the place where Cherie Blair most probably conceived her unexpected fourth child. Surrounded by rolling hills in the tiny village of St Martin d'Oydes, the twelfth-century hideaway was where the Blairs spent the precious last week of their summer holiday." So, then, did French hats now fly in the Ariège welkin? I do not know. I can be sure about only one hat that flew at this new intelligence, and where it did it.

It did it in the Cricklewood welkin. The hat was mine. It flew, moreover, for some time, because it was a straw hat, and so before the breeze allowed it to spiral back to earth an entire scenario was able to fill the head that had worn the hat during the period which now inspired its flight. That period was two summers ago, when the head had worn the hat to protect itself from the fierce

Ariège sun. And the head had not only worn the hat in the charming garden in which the Blairs had walked, it had lain, hatless now, on the pillow on which the Blairs had slept. For the generous hosts of Mr and Mrs Blair are also dear friends of Mr and Mrs Coren, to whom they have been, on many occasions, no less generous.

How odd it was on Saturday to learn that we had slept in the selfsame bed in which new Labour's most pleasing initiative had been launched! Odd, not just because of the coincidence which had gummed the missus and me into a corner of history's scrapbook, but because we knew the bed so well. We knew it as a bed in which accidents – it is our great leader's own word – could so easily happen. It is a splendid bed, but while its equally splendid mattress has all the length and breadth and depth one could want, it also has dipth. The dipth is in the middle of the bed, which means that however far apart a couple start the night, they will at some point in that night be rolled into one another. This, you will say, need not of itself lead to accidents, the couple may be heavy sleepers, but you say it because you do not know the other thing about the bed which Mrs Coren and I share, as it were, with the Blairs. The other thing is that just across the road from the charming dormitory is a charming church whose charming clock boasts a bell so charming that it can't resist boasting about it every half an hour.

Combine charm and dipth and you will soon see how accidents might happen. Especially if you have spent a delightful day slumped in a comfy poolside lounger, getting all the snooze your body needs, and thereby incurring an even greater risk of exchanging the deep peace of the *chaise-longue* for the hurly-burly of the marriage bed.

So readers will now understand why I was not only, like all of them, happy for the Blairs, but also happy for the Corens. However, being readers as alert as they are happy, they will, I know, have spotted those two wases and wondered why they are not two ises. Am I not still happy? Well, for the Blairs, yes; for the Corens, no. Because it is not Saturday now, it is Monday, and the PM has just announced that the likeliest spot was neither Tuscany nor France, but Balmoral. So does this mean that headgear is currently soaring over Buckingham Palace?

I wouldn't know. It's a fair way from Cricklewood, as the crown flies.


# *Float of the Bumblebee*


FORGIVE me, but I fear that this chunk of taradiddle is about to become even more unsettlingly intimate, for both of us, than the last. Then, you were required to join Mr and Mrs Coren in the bed of Mr and Mrs Blair. Now, we are in the bath together. You and I, that is: Mrs Coren is not in the bath with us; and the First Couple have never, as far as I know, been in it, but that is not to say that you and I are alone. It isn't you who is currently tickling my navel. It is a bumblebee.

It is a big bumblebee. It is as big as bumblebees get. I have not measured it between thumb and forefinger, because to do that I should have to move, and you will understand why that is something I would not want to do, but I am in a position to tell you – a position in which I have been petrified for the past five minutes – that the bee, observed horizontally, is roughly four square navels in area. Luckily. If it were an ordinary bee, less than one square navel in area, the area it would be in now would be my navel. I am widely read, and was in the Scouts, but I would not know how to get a bee out of a navel. Not that I know how to get a bee off a navel it is merely straddling but at least, if my racking brain does come up with something, it won't involve any poking about. This is not a bee you'd want to provoke.

For this is a kamikaze bee. All bumblebees, I know, sting and die, but they do not do this unless terminally provoked. They do not fly off, each dawn, on a suicide mission. Something tells me, however, that this bee is not as other bees are: when it flew in through the bathroom window a few minutes ago, it did not, as bees generally do, bounce buzzing off the walls until it found its entry point and buzz off, it circled above my head, buzzed once, and dived straight into the bath. It was as if Peter Snow, in one of his miniaturist demonstrations, were reconstructing the Battle of Midway. It could well be that the sound I heard as the bee launched its suicidal plunge was not a buzz at all but a bonsai "Banzai!"

If it had scored a direct hit, I should not be telling you this tale. Not because the sting would have killed me, but because the shock would have made me drop my titchy tape-recorder into the bath. I always have it with me, as I soak and mull, to murmur stuff for later transcription. But this stuff, as you will have noted from its present tense (and believe me, nobody is presently more tense than I) isn't being transcribed later: I am telling it like it is. This is now. I do not know what will happen next.

So, until we discover that together, let me fill you in on what I do know happened, after the bee hit the water. It did not sink; it bounced. It bounced on to my chest. It then tried to take off again, but its wings were wet, so it stopped, after a cheesed-off buzz or two, and grew very still, throbbing gently. It seemed to be taking stock of its surroundings. It was knee-deep in hair, but I do not know whether it knew that it was hair that it was knee-deep in: it had landed in Brobdingnag, but did it know what it had landed on? A patch of coarse brown sedge, or an inhabitant? Did it have a way of working it out? Despite wide reading and a woodcraft badge, I did not know whether bees recognised a soapy human being when they landed on one, if the human being was smart enough not to move or shriek or pre-empt any stinging with an ad hoc infarct, but I could tell that the bee was beginning to explore the possibility when, having now walked to the nearest nipple and climbed it, it then walked to the next one and just looked at it. This bee was thinking. So was I. I was thinking: this is a big bee, ergo an old bee, it has knocked about a bit, it may have seen nipples before, it may now be putting one and one together. And if so, will it strike?

It did not. Instead, it slowly trundled off, due south and eventually arrived where this narrative began, a few minutes ago, at my navel. Any minute now, it will walk

97

on. Don't worry, I hear you cry, this is a bath, your southern half must be underwater, it is safe from bees; but you do not know what I know. I know that I have been meaning to get this plug fixed for months. It is not a snug fit. You cannot lie in this bath for as long as the bee has forced me to without ending up in the two inches of water once demanded by wartime restrictions. And the enemy is at the gates.

# Forty Years On

THERE are two things for which we must not blame Stephen Winkley, the distinguished Headmaster of Uppingham School. First, we must not blame him for chairing the Boarding Education Alliance, a pressure group committed to reversing the decline in residential schools, since that is a perfectly proper ambition for someone who does not want to end up as a distinguished seller of *The Big Issue*. And second, we must not blame him, in his attempt to realise that ambition, for grasping the wrong end of the stick, since headmasters have not been permitted even to touch sticks for so many years now that the art of actually grasping them has inevitably fallen into tragic desuetude.

We may blame him only for not consulting me first, before he allowed Monday's *Times* to quote him as hoping that what he called "the Harry Potter effect" might reverse the decline, because "most of the children you meet have come across the books, and there is a sense that boarding is quite exciting and fun". No stick-end could be wronger, but still we cannot blame him, for his life requires him to meet too many children, and not enough middle-aged men. That is why he should have consulted me: because I meet large numbers of middle-aged men and they have all not merely come across the Harry Potter books, they are besotted with them; which is how I know which end of the stick to grasp.

Picture this. We are looking at several hundred acres of lushly rolling English greensward planted with ancient hardwood groves and copses, a sylvan paradise no individual middle-aged man could afford, any more than he could afford the magnificent mansion for which this landscape is the setting, or the enormous staff essential to the upkeep of both. Nevertheless, individual middle-aged men are snoozing on the sunlit grass, or reading in the shade of the trees, or flying kites and model aeroplanes; though they do, when the mood takes them, become less individual, by strolling across to one another to talk of this or that, and laugh. Still less individual ones are playing cricket on one or other of the several beautifully maintained pitches; they are not playing it well, being middle-aged and variously fat, arthritic, myopic, breathless, deaf, and so cack-handed that none would ever get into any club or village team, but they are enjoying themselves hugely. Others are playing bad tennis, or worse golf, or, on the immaculate running-track, attempting to break the four-minute furlong, while others yet are splashing happily about in the huge swimming pool, unconcerned at revealing either bodies which embarrassment keeps clad on youthful beaches, or the aquatic repertoire of a very old dog.

Until a dinner bell tolls, calling these hundreds of middle-aged chums into a fine vaulted hall, not to face pan-fried squid-liver and cappuccino of morelles followed by three roast elderberries in a kumquat coulis at a hundred quid a head, but wondrous sausage and mash, with spotted dick and custard for afters. Platters licked – and left for staff to clear – the happily bloated slope off for a Havana behind the bike shed, a scotch or three in the boiler room, a frame of snooker, a hand of bridge, a tryst with Lara Croft in the computer lab or a cackle with Jim Davidson on the common-room telly, until it is time to be tucked up in their dormitory beds by matron, perchance to dream of her lavendered bosom, perchance to lie awake swopping dirty jokes, perchance to open a sash on the offchance that a bit of a goer from the middle-aged ladies' college down the road has got over the wall, or, alternatively, to engage in something for which, in the unenlightened schools of their youth, they would have been summarily expelled, but need no longer fear.

And to awake, refreshed, to tuck in, unhectored by wife or quack, to a giga-cholesterol fried breakfast, and thence to classrooms for further voracious gobbling, this time of all the stuff they neglected – ruefully now – to learn as boys, but always swore they would one day catch up on, yet, life being life, somehow never got around to.

Grasp my end of the stick, Dr Winkley. Doesn't it feel good? Doesn't it suddenly lurch and point, like a dowser's hazel, to thousands of candidates eager to

100

cough up thousands in fees to revive the boarding schools? Trust it. All you have to do is raise the entry age to 60.

# Running Out of Puff

IF this morning, I tell you that my heart aches and a drowsy numbness pains my sense, you will probably nod smugly, knowing my little ways, and say, yes, there we go, he has been overdosing on nicotine again, he has been up half the night smoking, he has only himself to blame, he will get no sympathy from us, it is a filthy habit, look at his fingers, sniff his hair, check his ceiling, clock his clothes.

But while you would be unarguably right on all counts, you would still not have got anywhere near the nub of this particular aching numbness, since it is both different from the matutinal norm, and immeasurably worse; for while I have indeed been up half the night smoking, that is because I have been up half the night worrying about smoking. More particularly, about the serious effect smoking might henceforth have on me: for what really aches my heart and numbs my sense this fateful morning is that, after six unflaggingly loyal decades, I may never again rise to my feet for the national anthem, never again put folding money on this royal nag or that against the odds, never again raise my fedora as I pass Buck House, never again, at some formal dinner-table, wait respectfully until the loyal toast before lighting up, nor, at some more contentious one, ask a republican to step outside and repeat that. For although the monarchy has been not merely a lifelong habit with me but also a pleasure, a support, and a solace, I am now seriously thinking of giving it up. That is because, in the shattering decision she just taken to withdraw the royal warrant from cigarette manufacturers, the Queen – no, make that the queen; if I have not yet given up, at least let me cut down – has turned her back on me.

And what makes that rejection more bitter yet is that it was none other than she who had always sustained me against the manifold rejections of all the rest: what did I care if theatres and cinemas barred their doors against me, or cabbies threw me out, or doctors struck me off, or public transport belied its name, or chic restaurants directed me to the manky chip shops opposite, or airlines reduced my transglobal dreams to short-hop nightmares, or even dear friends said would you mind awfully… what did any of this matter when, back on the lonely pavement, I could slip from my coat pocket a pack of Silk Cut whose titchy golden escutcheon would catch the moonlight, lion and unicorn rampant to assure me that what I was about to ignite had been personally appointed by my sovereign lady? Not smoke? Dear God, it seemed an act of treason to abstain!

More yet, my gratitude for this approval led me to honour all the rest of her endorsements. While other anxious shoppers trolleyed the supermarket aisles, squinting at e-numbers, additives, substitutes, sell-by dates, fat contents, mineral deposits, national provenances, political rectitudes, and umpteen other boons and threats, I have never sought any signal but one. Enter my larder and you will find only her gracious marmalade, her regal fish paste, her sovereign cereal, her radiant sauce.

What is my scullery but a little shrine to her palate? A place of not just devotion but, yes, communion: oft in the stilly night, when I have tiptoed down for a cold beef sandwich and a glass of stout, a devoted tear has pricked my eye at the thought that, just a few miles up the road, she herself might, at that very moment, be spreading the self-same mustard on the self-same bread, and raising the self-same nectar to her lip.

But that's all over, now. Even as I write, the Master of the Queen's Fagges, ordained to sample the market in her service, is glumly stuffing his bits and bobs into his gunny-sack while he waits for his P45 to come down from upstairs, no doubt recalling with a heavy heart those jolly weekly exchanges – "Are one's ciggies still full of flavour?', "Unquestionably ma'am, and as firmly packed as ever"; "And the tips sufficiently corky?'; "Indeed so, Your Majesty, and a snip at the price"... doomed now to be naught but a secret between him and the tabloid press; and it is therefore time for me, in my turn, to go down and clear out my larder.

Odd, that it should be exactly 400 years since Walter Raleigh taught a grateful queen to smoke. Though it pains me deeply to say it, they don't, I fear, make Elizabeths like they used to.

# Can We Get There By Candlelight?

MILLIONS of my devoted readers will have been deeply rattled by Monday's news that the best-selling card this Christmas cocks a major snook at everything they are devoted to. On this millennial cusp, it does not show the birthday baby, it does not show hovering angels, it does not show adoring shepherds, it does not even show a star in the bright sky. What it shows is a hungover reindeer with its head down a lavatory.

Hardly surprising, then, that I should have taken my phone off the hook. I cannot have millions of devoted readers jamming the Cricklewood switchboards in their desperate search for an explanation of why it is that the nation's favourite yuletide icon should now be a sozzled Lapp ruminant losing its lunch. But nor can I have them left in red-eyed bewilderment, simply because their lifelong devotion to one version of the Christmas story has kept them ignorant of the other. I shall have to tell them about The Three Dim Men.

Now when Jesus was born in Bethlehem of Judaea in the days of Herod the king, behold, there came not only three wise men from the east to Jerusalem, there also came three dim men from the east who never got to Jerusalem at all. They were so dim that they were incapable not merely of reading a map, but of deciding which star to follow, since there seemed to be a lot of bright ones about; so they plumped for the North Star because it looked as though it belonged to a giant saucepan, and two of the dim men reckoned this could be a sign from God. It is true that the third dim man did inquire why God would choose a saucepan as a sign, but he shut up when told by the others that God moved in mysterious ways.

Thus, after many long and arduous months journeying north, they eventually crossed the Arctic Circle – devoted readers may at last understand something that has been puzzling them for years, viz T S Eliot's opening of *The Journey of the Magi*, in which one dim man says "A cold coming we had of it," because devoted readers couldn't figure out why Palestine should be cold – and arrived at what is now Trond. It was also Trond then (not much changes in Lapland ) and had the one inn it still has, where they decided to stop; for the North Star, since they were so far north, was slap-bang over the inn. Unfortunately, the inn was full – as it always is, because it is so cold in Lapland that once people find a warm room, they move in permanently – but the landlord twigged that the three men were so dim that they would pay top dollar for anything. He realised this because their first words to him were: "Where is he that is born King of the Jews?" and the landlord knew you would have to be really dim to think there were any Jews in Lapland, so he said: "He is out back in the Royal Suite, which you can share with him for only 80 krons a night, plus 65 per cent service."

He then showed his three guests to the stable. And it was there, as they peered into a gloom even dimmer than they were, that they spotted a manger, with something eating from it. They had never seen anything like their new room-mate before. Their first thought was that it was a horse wearing a hat-rack, but as their eyes grew accustomed to the light, they realised that the horns were actually growing out of its head; and though none of the dim men had ever seen a Jew, it was common knowledge that Jews had horns, and they therefore concluded that they had indeed found what they had sought for so long. Whereupon they fell to their knees, adored for a bit, and then proffered the reindeer the gifts each of them had brought: gin, whisky, and advocaat, because a bottle is always acceptable. The reindeer, however, merely went on eating, without looking up, leaving the three dim men to agree that this was a pretty majestic way to behave, and proof if proof were needed; so they opened the bottles, and poured them into the manger.

With the inevitable consequence that, after about half an hour, the reindeer finally raised its head, stared glassily at the three dim men, walked into the wall, and threw up. Which is why, two millennia on, this has become such a traditional way of celebrating that people prefer sending a card commemorating it to any other. I haven't seen one mind, so I don't know if it also wishes you a Merry Christmas. But I do.

# Widdecombe Fare

SOME of you may find it a mite spooky that, in all the
many hundreds of tête-à-têtes which we have shared
over the years, I have never once mentioned that I was a
bit clairvoyant. You are the some, of course, who are
yourselves a bit clairvoyant, and who have murmured, at
this moment or that, out of the blue, "something tells me
he's a bit clairvoyant". The rest of you have never given
it a second thought, because, lacking the gift, you never
gave it the first one; so it is to you in particular that I
address myself today, partly because you are the ones
who need convincing, partly because the others already
know what I am going to say.

I am going to say that, for several days now, you have
been wondering about Ann Widdecombe: Uncanny, eh?
It gets better: I can even tell you what you were
wondering. You were wondering whether, when last
week she declared to the new Register of MPs' Interests
that she had been given a bent BBC teaspoon, the
Shadow Health Secretary was simply being scrupulously
honest, or whether she was, less simply, deploying
honesty unscrupulously in order to wind everybody up.
Well, I am here to gainsay both options; and I am here to
do it because I was there to do it, on the afternoon of 10
December 1998, in the hospitality suite of BBC Pebble
Mill in Birmingham, whither the *dramatis personae*
involved had convened to play *Call My Bluff*, and thus
where Miss Widdecombe met, for the first time, Mr Uri
Geller.

It was, in every sense, a magic moment. As their team captain, it had fallen to me to introduce my two illustrious guests to one another, and I have to say that nothing less than the aptly metaphysical John Donne will suffice to describe what happened next: their eye-beames twisted, and did thredde their eyes upon one double string. More astonishing yet, each was, quite literally, gobsmacked by the other: eerily enwrapped, the two people in the country hitherto least likely to be lost for words, found not a one. You could have heard a pin bend. And then, uncannily – until you recall that he is as clairvoyant a cove as you can shake a Ouija board at – Mr Geller divined precisely what Miss Widdecombe was thinking, picked up a BBC teaspoon from the table beside them, held it aloft between thumb and forefinger, and made it droop.

Whereupon the Shadow Home Secretary slowly raised her own thumb and forefinger – I cannot swear they were not trembling – gently took the buckled cutlery, and placed it reverently in her handbag. After which she no less gently took, by the elbow, Mr Geller himself, sat beside him on a sofa strategically placed to serve momentous historical happenings, and listened while he talked. And how he talked! And how she listened! They might have been Othello and Desdemona, he rabbiting on about anthropophagi and men whose heads do grow beneath their shoulders, she letting herself be bowled over by his wondrous stories into helpless captivation. I did not, of course, eavesdrop on all that was said, but from the disparate fragments gleaned as I refilled a cup or offered egg-and-cress, I could sense that a self-portrait was emerging, despite his fabled modesty, of a man of both great spiritual depth and great material achievement, a man able to read and memorise ten books in a morning before transporting himself across the planet in nano-seconds to heal the inexplicably sick, pluck a global corporation from the red, dowse unerringly for oil and bauxite, adjust an errant satellite, and all this without first dashing into a phonebox to move his Y-fronts to the outside.

Okay, you say, you claim to be a bit of a clairvoyant, so what was the wide-eyed Miss Widdecombe thinking while Uri was telling her all this? Okay, I reply, she was thinking: here is an internationally recognised byword with a full head of lustrous hair and not a trace of either paunch or dubious Yorkshire accent, who has risen to transglobal heights of wealth and popularity by per-suading countless millions that he can perform miracles; here is a glamour-puss who could not only cut NHS waiting lists at a stroke by the laying-on of hands in a thousand places at once and raise education standards to the top of the international league by telepathising the speed-read *Britannica* into every infant brain, but also repair every voter's clock, tumble-drier and toaster just by grinning at them from the TV screen and snapping his fingers.

Voters? Oh yes. That is what she was thinking. She was thinking: here, at last, is a true leader. That is why she has declared her interest. We shall hear more of this anon. Mark my words. Watch this spoon.

# Lover's Leap

*D*EAR *Stella Young:*

The first object of this letter is, of course, to wish you a rapid and complete recovery. I do apologise for tendering that wish so publicly, but when I rang Taunton Hospital this morning to inquire after your condition, the charming staff nurse on Gould Ward told me that you were coming along a treat and would be leaving in a day or two. There was therefore no point in sending you a get-well card to reach you after you had got well enough not to receive it, and today's newspapers have neglected to publish your home address. Not, mind, that your home would be all that difficult to find, since Stogursey is, I understand, a small village, and if I addressed the card to you at The House With a Human Catapult in the Garden, I imagine that the postman would be able to work things out for himself; but it seemed in poor taste.

The second object of this letter is to assure you that, despite what insensitive tongues may be saying, you are not nuts. You are a deeply caring woman, alert to your partner's every need. If the man in your life is a keen member of the Dangerous Sports Club and has spent two arduous years of his own life in building a wooden catapult designed to hurl a woman 70 feet above her back garden at 50 mph in order to land her in a net 150 feet away, true love dictates your only course. Should that course go a bit wonky and you bounce out of the net and break your pelvis in umpteen places, it is a small price to pay. Indeed, I know that you already know this, for you are the esteemed manager of the Bridgwater Citizens Advice Bureau, and on more than one occasion must have professionally advised citizens in cases not dissimilar from your own: were, say, a member of the Dangerous Animals Club to front up at your office, saying that his wife had lost her taste for sticking her head in their lion's mouth, I am sure you would have a sharp word with the woman regarding love, honour and obedience; just as you would, I know, do your very best to save any marriage in which one spouse had inconsiderately refused to try jumping from roof to moving roof across the M5 for a bet large enough to enable the other spouse to wipe his slate clean in the bar of the Dangerous Wagers Club.

But this letter has a third object, too. It is to reassure you, dear Mrs Young, that my reassurances are worth the paper they are printed on, in this case 35p of anybody's money, for I have been there, too. My partner, like yours, is a boundlessly imaginative and inventive spirit who throughout our many years together has come up with innumerable dare-devil theories in the practical proof of which I have been only too happy to assist her. We had hardly embarked upon life's happy path together indeed, before she excitedly came to me with a theory she had been working on that a degree in English Literature qualified a man to put up a greenhouse without the need of a Royal Free Hospital surgeon to repair a severed tendon in his left arm.

Better yet, as undaunted by her slight miscalculation as, say, Leonardo da Vinci would have been had he built a bicycle wearing a mysterious smile, she went on to

111

develop the theory – worked out with a mathematical precision which, 20 years on, still leaves me in undiluted awe – that, if it took two professional roofers six days to replace the tiles on a partly dodgy roof at £12 an hour each, then it would cost far less for one professional hack to do the same job however long it took. That it took only ten minutes for the roof to become so wholly dodgy that it ended up on the ground not merely alongside but all over the hack, thus now requiring two professional roofers for 12 days at £12 an hour each, served only to increase my admiration for a brilliant tactician whose eagerness to put her theories to the test, irrespective of the practical consequences, marked her out as one whose imagination was surpassed only by her courage.

And, more touchingly still, by her unswerving faith in her partner. For, however bizarre the theory over which she has been racking her untiring brain, I am the first person to whom she invariably, and loyally, turns to test it. Might it be possible to unblock a drain by binding bamboo canes together until they are long enough to break off and require the tester to get down in the manhole and, slipping, bring the manhole cover down on him? Could man's eternal quest to put up a porch-light without fusing himself to the National Grid ever be achieved? Should all blowlamps be built to point one way, all chainsaws banned, all hammers come with thumb-proof heads?

Hers to ponder, mine to test. That, Stella, is the way it is in the Dangerous Marriage Club.

# London Belongs To Me

I'M off to the Dome, me. Any minute now. Just a few things to be sorted out first, and then I'm away to Greenwich. That is the joy of living in London, it is not like living in Runcorn or Bute, you do not have to engage in major long-term plans and serious expenditure if you want to take in the sights, you do not have to pore over timetables or work out complex routes, you do not have to book expensive hotels or give advance notice to employers or arrange with neighbours to feed the cat and water the pot plants, you do not have to turn off the gas and notify the police of keyholders, or pack for unpredictable meteorological contingencies, you just walk out of your gate and, a short bus ride away, there it all is – ships, towers, domes, theatres and temples lie, open unto the fields and to the sky, all bright and glittering in the smokeless air. Any time you choose, you can go. Everything is always there.

Like the Tower of London. It has been there since 1038. As early as 1947, I nearly went, my sandwiches were packed, the Tizer was in my satchel, the school bus was ticking over at the corner of Cecil Road, but then I sneezed a couple of times, and she was always a worrier, my mother. But no matter, the Tower would always be there, the Crown Jewels, the ravens, the Beefeaters, the Traitor's Gate, a terrific day out, and I shall certainly get around to it any day now. I have of course seen it many times and not just driving past, either: I stopped once, got out, and had a look in the moat. It is a really knockout moat. It made me more determined than ever to do a proper visit, sometime.

I could do it on the day I visit the Monument, it is a stone's throw away, you could kill two birds with that stone, it is merely a matter of deciding whether to go up the Monument first or afterwards. There is an amazing view from the top, tourists come from all over the globe, but you have to climb 365 steps to get to it, and that could take time. I might be too knackered for the Tower, after that. I intended to go with David Collingwood in 1951, the year we didn't go to the Festival of Britain; I actually had a golf ball in my pocket, we we're going to drop it off the Monument to see how high it would bounce, but we went to the pictures instead. I'm not even sure I could do 365 steps now, it would be a bit embarrassing to drop dead at step 189, it is a spiral staircase, the emergency services would have a hell of a job getting a stretcher all that way up and down, they might have to lug me to the top and lower me on a rope. An undignified way to go. Not nice for the family.

St Paul's would be a safer bet. There is only one flight of steps up to the famed Whispering Gallery. God knows what's held me back all these years, but I shall of course go, as soon as I've thought of something a bit special to whisper. A man in my position can't whisper any old rubbish. Ears on the other side would expect to hear a joke. The smart thing to do would be to practise in Guildhall, it doesn't have an echo; at least, I don't think it does, but it'd be a doddle to find out, it is only a half-hour bus ride from Cricklewood and you would also get to see the world's most magnificent municipal building. Still, it's been there since 1430, it is unlikely to fall down over the next few days, there's no rush, I could go after I've visited Westminster Abbey, which has poets underneath it. You can stand on Chaucer. Better still, I could make a day of it by walking from the abbey across Horse Guards Parade on the day Her Majesty was Trooping the Colour, it looks terrific on television, and then visit Buckingham Palace, open to the public now, and an absolute must. I just hope the Millennium Wheel is working by June, it is a mere stroll from the Palace, it'd be crazy to miss the opportunity, the bit of the wheel you can see from my roof looks stunning. You can also see the Post Office Tower and Canary Wharf, both essential to go to the top of for unparalleled views of the world's greatest city, which I eagerly look forward to, even if you can't see Peter Pan's statue, one of my top priorities. I shall visit it very soon, also the Serpentine, which I've often nearly seen, only to be irritatingly thwarted by having to fasten my seat-belt and make sure my tray-table was safely stowed.

And, after all that, the Dome awaits. Why my heart leaps within me at the very prospect, who can say? Maybe it's because I'm a Londoner.

# *Mouse Trap*

FOR the time being, this column is being written by me. But the time being what it is, it may not be long before this column is being written by a mouse. It is, mind, being partly written by a mouse already, in so far as I employ a mouse to help me out with it: the mouse is, of course, the little grey gofer wired into my computer which, when I push it around and poke it (I am a fair employer, but firm) dutifully carries out the little humdrum tasks which are its lot in life. It does what I tell it. It never puts in its two penn'orth. It does not have a mind of its own.

But all that is about to change; and though it is about to change for the immeasurable worse, there is nothing I can do to stop it. For, according to *The Sunday Times*, a Californian company is poised to launch a smart mouse which interacts with its employer, irrespective of whether its employer wishes to be interacted with or not. This new mouse does not just umbilically serve its computer, it embodies a titchy computer of its own, equipped with a battery of sensors designed to monitor the finger poking it about and tell it when to stop doing it. The sensors react to stress, fatigue, sickness, and any other of the thousand natural shocks that flesh is heir to, and if they don't like what they sense is exuded by that flesh, they instantly flash their findings on to the screen and tell their employer he is in no shape to carry on. More nightmarish yet, if they deem his state to be grave enough, they may shut his computer down, for what their professional opinion considers to be his own good. Which is to say that if I were working with one of these mice this morning, I would not have got this far, since I have a touch of Sydney Bug – I see him, such is the delirium induced by a temperature of 102, as a leathery little bacterium in a cork-hung hat and smelly flip-flops who doesn't give a XXXX for anyone else – and my mouse, halfway through my first sweated sentence, would have ordered me to gobble a fistful of paracetamol and crawl under my duvet until the NHS was in a position to find my remains a refrigerated truck.

But why, you ask, need that ever happen to me, when I have a perfectly good mouse that goes about its business without getting any ideas above its station? Because one day it will cease to be perfectly good – I have got through four mice already, I have a heavy forefinger – and it is an immutable law of cybernetics that anything which goes phut can be replaced only by something newer which the industry wants to flog you. Any time now, I shall have no choice but to couple destinies with a mouse committed to making my life hell. We shall be Tom and Jerry.

And you may be sure that Jerry will not stop at merely ordering me to chuck in the sponge if he spots a touch of flu. One morning, perhaps, having noted a slight rise in blood pressure, he will refuse to operate unless I give up fags immediately; or he will insist, having performed a covert liver function test, that I spend the rest of my life on barley water; or he will spot that I am leaning ever closer towards my screen, surf the Internet for an ophthalmologist seeking to treat himself to a new Ferrari, and book me into the London Clinic for a cataract operation that same afternoon, securing its penthouse suite, thanks to my credit card details, with an unrefundable deposit composed mainly of noughts.

Do you wonder that I felt hit by both barrels when I read on Monday of the AOL-Time Warner merger? This $350 billion agglomerate having ensured that everything purchasable in the world is to be at Jerry's www fingertips, how will I ever be able to foresee all the consequences of poking him with mine? Halfway through a piece designed simply to kill a few of your minutes and pay a few of my bills, the mouse may, if I pause too long in my choice of adverb, summarily diagnose work-related stress, and, not content just to wipe my jottings from the screen and replace them with a soothing MGM musical, order up a magnum of Valium, dispatch a squad of aromatherapists to my door, book me a Concorde-borne month in Barbados, and hand in my notice to *The Times*.

Unless, of course, I end up with six tons of anthracite, a treble-glazed loft extension, and a century's sub-scription to *Reader's Digest*. In cyberspace, the best-laid schemes o' mice an' men gang aft a-gley.

# On a Wing and a Prayer

IT is manifestly clear that, despite the most stalwart and selfless efforts on the part of the press, the television, the Government, the Opposition, the BMA, the drug manufacturers, the Health & Safety Executive, the care industry, and peers with big black moustaches, there are still not nearly enough new health scares coming on to the market. Some days, indeed, so few fresh terrors are reported that countless hypochondriacs besiege GP surgeries and hospital casualty departments complaining of Neurosis Deprivation Syndrome, putting tremendous pressures on the collapsing NHS to think up the name of a NDS miracle cure not yet available in this country – despite its success in making American mice believe they are terminally ill – so that patients can be reassured that they really might have something to worry about.

Hats off, then (provided, of course, you are not standing near anyone or anything likely to infect an uncovered head with a new strain of something) to Mr Farrol Kahn of the Aviation Health Institute. Did you know there was an Aviation Health Institute? Well, ye ken noo. It is based in Oxford, and its latest contribution to driving people nuts is, announced AHI director Kahn yesterday, a £10 surgical mask to protect air travellers from bacteria and viruses floating around aircraft cabins. These respirators, he declares, will block 98 per cent of all bugs. What he does not declare is that this will make the surviving two per cent so evolutionarily hearty that the day cannot be far off when they will be able to punch holes in the fuselage and blow the entire masked company into the stratosphere; but that is a scare for tomorrow, when, I am confident, the AHI will be able to come up with a miracle antidote, such as going by boat.

What I am less confident about is Mr Kahn's restraint in suggesting that, when we all fly off into the wide blue yonder, sitting there in respirators will be enough. True, on short-haul flights, the impediment of a gas mask may dissuade travellers from eating in-flight food, thereby protecting them from all the terminal things you can catch off a slice of nineteenth-century corned beef and a toenail of GM tomato, but long-haul passengers will have to eat, and Mr Kahn should surely have addressed the attendant serious risks. Merely struggling with a packet of airline peanuts can dislocate a wrist or result in your neighbour being felled by an elbow to the jaw, possibly both, just as finally opening a titchy pot of UHT milk can spray an entire row with something which, after a few incubating hours in a hot cabin, could well transmute into brucellosis or CJD. Surely, Mr Kahn, we should all be fed through an intravenous drip and compelled to wear hermetically sealed boiler suits or – on Go or Easyjet – Sellotaped binliners? Especially given the bonus: our protection, should our drowsing neighbour slump against our shoulder, from anything infectious lurking in his dribble.

For passengers condemned to window seats, a sturdy reinforced nose cowl should be worn above the mask. Too often, when the captain announces that if you turn to the right you will see Mont Blanc, the eager alp-enthusiast will find that his conk has collided with the

120

window. Should a nose-bleed result, he might, in these haemophobic times, find himself summarily removed by stewards in latex gloves and chucked in the luggage hold. Aisle-seat passengers would, of course, wear shoulder-guards to shield fragile scapulae from trolley-jolt.

As for rubber boots, Mr Kahn, I'm staggered that an amateur like me should be the one to suggest them. Have you never used either of the two lavatories designed to serve 300 passengers compelled to queue for so long that their bladders end up throbbing like a ship's boiler? With the result that when you do finally force your way into the cubicle – and if you'd like another handy tip, Mr Kahn, stout gardening gloves will protect forefingers from sliding bolts likely to shear them off at the knuckle – you find your intercontinental haven to be ankle-deep in incontinental fluid. To say nothing of that wodge of discoloured Kleenex in the sink which is almost certainly giving off enough germs to put a town the size of Huddersfield into intensive care. Forgive my criticisms of the AHI, Mr Kahn, but I trust you catch my drift. If you catch anything else, you have only yourself to blame.

# How Does Your Garden Grow?

O N my lawn there are 48 snowdrops. I counted them all in, last September, and, last week, I counted them all out. Hardly a heart-stopping horticultural triumph, you will say, nothing to preen about, these are not 48 black tulips, these are not 48 blue Himalayan poppies, these are not 48 epidendrum ilemse orchids, these are not 48 titan arum lilies, nobody at Kew will be turning cartwheels at your news, nobody at *The Guinness Book of Records* will be stopping presses, nobody from the BBC Natural History Unit will be frantically caning their OB vans down the M4 from Bristol – because everyone knows that the way to get 48 snowdrops is to poke your finger in your lawn 48 times, pop in 48 tiddly bulbs, and wait for the snowdrop gene to strut its stuff.

Don't be so sure. Everyone who claims to know this is living in the innocent lang syne, when snowdrops which went in as bulbs came out as flowers. Now they come out as bulbs. Ask Chief Superintendent Steve Parnell of the Cambridgeshire Constabulary, the nation's snowdrop czar, who has just circulated the names and details of known bulb rustlers to every force in Britain. Better yet, ask two of the rustlers, banged up a couple of weeks back for stripping a Hertfordshire wood of 300,000 snow-drops. A wood, let me say, not ten short miles from Crickle's: had they not been caught bulbhanded, their tally might well have been 300,048 by now. That is why I feel entitled to claim a triumph. That is why I look on my 48 snowdrops with pride.

It is also why I look on them all the time. They are the first thing I look on in the morning, and they are the last thing I look on at night; because after I have given Mr Paxman a reciprocal nod, locked up, set the burglar alarm, brushed my teeth, wound my watch, and done one press-up, I go out on the landing again, flash my torch at the garden, and count. Then I put the torch on my bedside table, because, despite Chief Superintendent Parnell's entreaties to my local nick, you never know: if I wake to a creaking fence in the middle of the night, a neighbouring bark, I am out on the landing in a trice, raking the garden with everything that Duracell can throw at it. It is like Colditz.

And this is only February. The snowdrops are mere harbingers. There are croci and bluebells and narcissi and daffs and tulips to come, or more probably go. To say nothing of the wizened tubers in the garage: I used to worry about thieves stepping on the dahlias to get to the car, now I worry about them stepping on the car to get to the dahlias. God knows how the owners are getting through the night at such marginally flashier backyards as Sissinghurst or Wisley or Hidcote: are there Serious Bulb Squad dobermanns in every potting shed, are the trees heavy with camouflaged SAS men waiting, at the first squelch of an illicit trowel, to abseil down, flinging stun grenades and squirting Stens? What are curators doing at Kiftsgate, which boasts the nation's biggest, oldest rose? It may be 80 ft high and 100 ft long, but if an entire wood can be de-bulbed in a night, Filipes Rosa Kiftsgate could be uprooted in a trice, galloped across the lawn like a giant floral centipede, juggernauted down to Southampton to catch the morning tide, and find itself, a scant week later, gracing the grotto of whichever Colombian drug baron put in the highest bid. All things considered, I wouldn't hold out much hope for Hampton Court Maze, either: any day now, it will be straddling the grounds of some enormous Sicilian villa, its privet labyrinths full of bemused Mafiosi irritably trying to shoot their way out.

Can there be a reason for this sudden upsurge in botanical theft? Can there be anyone responsible? Not half, there can. Like fresh turf, the blame can be laid fairly and squarely at the feet of Alan Titchmarsh and Charlie Dimmock and Carol Vorderman and Monty Don and Gay Search and Ali Ward and Anne McKevitt and all the other hortimaniac quick-fixers who have sprouted and burgeoned and infested every television channel, and who, not only instantly makeover domestic scrublands into dinky floral treats but are also shown doing it in jocular fast-action. They are Mack Sennett's Keystone Gardeners, and what they have generated is not a love of horticulture but a love of haste. What do we want? A perfect garden! When do we want it? Now!

# Auto Suggestion

FOR this morning's disappointment, I have only myself to blame. Two long years packed to the Whitehall gunwales with tough new guidelines and radical new initiatives, to say nothing of tough new initiatives and radical new guidelines, should by now have taught me to decode such tonibabble into the waffling bumf it invariably is. I should have known that when the Driving Standards Agency this morning cried "Tarrah!" and announced "fresh initiatives and tougher guidelines to make the driving test more in keeping with the current driving culture", it had done nothing of the sort. It had merely lifted the battered bonnet of the existing test, fiddled with this, tinkered with that, run an oily rag over the points, slammed the lid shut, and pushed the clapped out old banger back on to the homicidal road. All the DSA has done is require learners to look in their mirrors a bit more, stall a bit less, make fewer nine-point turns, reverse into fewer lamp-posts, and ensure that fewer old ladies shout "Oy!" on zebra crossings. They will then be kissed on both cheeks, and allowed to use the prefix 007.

Do you wonder at my sunken heart? Having trawled my fine-toothed comb through the recommendations twice, I can find nothing at all in keeping with the current driving culture. Where, for example, is the filling-station stage of the test, now that garages are supermarkets with pumps? Should it not be incumbent upon any examiner to require his candidate to pull in, fill up, go inside to pay, and see what else he buys? Any learner buying food would be failed instantly. I have been passed on too many motorways by too many swerving drivers fiddling between their legs for a dropped Smartie or steering with their elbows while struggling to find the opening strip on a prawn sandwich not to know how essential it is to nip this practice in the learning bud. As to parent learners unable to resist buying their rear seat a couple of mirror-filling Teletubby balloons, an examiner should be allowed not merely to fail them, but to put their children into care immediately, both for their own safety and mine. I don't even want to think about any learner emerging with a cup of hot coffee to stand on his dashboard.

Nor is there anything in the guidelines about cassette-players. All examiners should be required to insert a tape which jams, and then hand the learner a pencil. If the learner starts poking the pencil about in the slot (even if not at a roundabout, where most drivers do it), he should be required to stop the car and go home by bus. The examiner should also pre-programme the radio with six stations the driver doesn't want, switch it on, and pass him the manual. Most drivers, in my experience, will want to prop this on the dashboard while in the fast lane, often simultaneously holding their cellphone between clavicle and ear in case they need to phone a friend to get the kiloherzage of Radio Brent.

And so to the enormous range of totally unnecessary in-car controls with which the current driving culture has blessed us. The fascia of even the cheapest models now enables a driver not only to regulate the climate so as to keep his chin warm and his nose cool while fresh air blows up one trouser-leg but not the other, he can also, at the touch of hardly more than three dozen buttons, check everything from the state of his brake-pads and the optimum speed of his headlamp wipers to whether his Trafficmaster recommends avoiding Knightsbridge and, if so, his coin-carrier contains sufficient meterage for Hampstead. Any learner daring even to glance down at these knobs would instantly fail.

Nothing in the guidelines about personalised number-plates, either. Odd, given that about 80 per cent of cars now bear them, almost every one so baffling as to risk suicidal distraction. 5EXY and Hl JOE are all very well, but I once followed a Transit van tagged NANIA for ten miles trying to see if it had a lion, a witch, and a wardrobe in the back, and became so preoccupied that I missed the Heathrow turn off, and my flight. Any learner pondering such things aloud would be immediately struck off.

A no less amazing omission, in the current driving culture, is a test for male learners overtaken on the inside, very quickly, by a girl in a Ferrari, or for females over-taken on the outside, very slowly, by a juggernaut with its co-driver's bare backside pressed to the window.

But most baffling of all is why is all this, and so much else, absent from the great initiative? Should we lay it at the foot of John Prescott, Trafficmaster supreme? I cannot say. I know only that whenever that foot is on the throttle of either of his Jaguars, I'd sooner be indoors.

# If I May Be Brief

This is the last column I shall write from the loft. Indeed, it may well be the last column I shall write from anywhere. Provided I finish it. If I do not finish it, it will just be the last words I shall write from anywhere – in which case you will not be reading it, because this is a quality newspaper and does not publish columns which end halfway through a sentence. Not that *The Times* would receive the words anyway, because if they ended halfway through a sentence I would be in no position to send them, since it would mean that I too had ended halfway through the sentence, and the position I would be in would be flat out beside the desk. That is why, in all our interests, I am doing my best to avoid this happening by typing very slowly.

I also, this morning, crept up to the loft very slowly. For the past 40 years, I have run up to the loft very quickly, because I thought it was good for me. It got the pulse racing; it got the adrenalin going. But I do not want my pulse to race any more, I want it to chug. Nor do I want to get my adrenalin going, because it might go altogether. You never know with adrenalin, if you are bald. I did not know you never knew that, mind, until yesterday, when I read it in this quality newspaper. I read that bald men were three times more likely to suffer a heart attack than hairy men. So says Harvard Medical School, and who am I to argue with them? If I argued with them I might get worked up, and if I got worked up, I could find myself proving their point. Or, rather, someone else could find me. I prefer to address the Harvard researchers' further observation that, "with vigilant attention, bald men can markedly reduce their risk". That is why I am now doing every thing very slowly.

If I may be brief – and, God knows, I may be – Harvard's research indicates that the increased cardiac risk to the bald derives from their having far higher levels of testosterone than the thatched, a bonus hitherto regarded by all slapheads as one of Mother Nature's little compensations. We now know it to be one of Mother Nature's little jokes. Indeed, it is confirmation of her role: if things were run by Father Nature, he would never have made it. The joke is that the more virile a man is, the riskier it is to exercise his virility. It is a sort of Hobson's choice – certainly if your name is Hobson and, your head being of the coot persuasion, your hormones tell you it is time to go three rounds with Mrs Hobson. You would, as a dutiful husband, be obliged to ring your solicitor first and ensure that your affairs were in order. You owe that much to the Widow Hobson. Then again, if she has taken the Harvard findings on board, she may herself not choose to risk it; it is all very well having the earth moved, but what if the place it moves to is over your loved one's mahogany lid?

As for less orderly affairs, I think we may assume that Hobson can kiss those goodbye. Henceforth it will be all he can kiss. Up until now, baldies have been smugly confident that their gleaming testosterone advertisement constituted an offer no sporting woman could refuse, but that will nevermore be the case. Even if Hobson were prepared to take his life in his hands by sidling up to Winona Ryder at Tesco's checkout and suggesting they

129

nip down to Bognor in his roadster, what likelihood is there, now, that she would leap at the chance, given the strong probability of her having to ring room service in the middle of the night and ask for an intensive care unit to be sent up to the bridal suite? That's if they get there at all: with only one of them having enough hair to be blown about in the MG's slipstream, the odds on the other one, in his palpitating anticipation, copping an infarct and suddenly leaving the M23 through the central reservation are, say Harvard, very short indeed. This is a bad business all round, for those of us with hair all round.

I have had nothing on top since the early Eighties, and never thought about it, until yesterday. Yesterday made me think about tomorrow. Especially as *The Times* report chose as its highlight quote: "A bare crown can carry an increased risk similar to that for smoking." Which means that a bald addict is six times likelier to have a heart attack. There is nothing for it: in future, if there is one, I shall just have to write downstairs and smoke very slowly.

# *Barking Mad*

For some 12 million happy residents of Britain, only 26 days of that happiness remain. They do not know this, mind, because a primary source of their happiness is that they never know what is going to happen next. They cannot see the future, and do not know it doesn't work. They have no idea that, from 28 February, their happy residence of Britain will nevermore be secure. From 28 February they will be able to go abroad.

More precisely, and more horribly, they will be able to be taken abroad. Whether they want to or not. They do not, of course, know whether they want to or not, because they do not know what abroad is. Nor can they be told: if you try to tell them what abroad is, they will just look at you, or look at something else. True, some of them may bark, others may miaow, but these replies cannot be taken to mean an understanding of abroad. They will not understand what abroad is until they get there, and then it will be too late.

Hitherto, British dogs and cats have had terrific holidays. When their owners went abroad, flinging themselves ever further in man's nympholeptic quest for vacational bliss, the dogs and cats were sent to delightful kennels and catteries in places like Frinton or Harrogate or Lytham St Anne's, where they were looked after by caring and knowledgeable hosts who fed them good British food and let them play in fresh British air and sleep in comfy British baskets, and introduced them to other British guests with whom they could happily mingle, exchange sound British views on this and that, and possibly enjoy, thanks to the rigorous surveillance of sturdy British landladies, innocent holiday romances that hurt nobody. They spent the kind of delightful prelapsarian fortnights no longer available to human Britons, except in period television whodunnits.

Not all British cats and dogs were sent away to hotels,

of course, many were allowed to stay in their own happy, familiar homes and were cared for by jolly neighbours who came round and fed them what they were used to eating and did not shout at them if they slept on their owners' beds or left hairs on their owners' sofas or brought mice in or chewed shoes or widdled on the rug, because jolly neighbours do not see discipline as their remit. They want only to be able to tell returning owners that their pet has not snuffed it.

But from 28 February, pets will not be able to have terrific holidays any more. They will get a nasty jab, a microchip, and a passport, and be shoved into the back of a car, whisked through a terrifying tunnel or decanted on to a bucking boat, and driven thousands of jolting kilometres to some broiling alien hell-hole full of indecipherable smells and enemy animals who don't understand them no matter how slowly and loudly they bark or miaow. They will share one small hot room with their masters, their food will be inedible, unfamiliar bugs will forage in fur and gut alike to induce nights sleepless with itching and retching, the pavements will fry their feet, and if they head for the shade, they will find out that the dachshunds have got there first. Always provided the shade is not on the other side of a road packed with traffic roaring from unfamiliar directions, in which case they will find themselves being peeled off, returned to the hotel, and slid under their owners' doors with a stiff note from the hall porter pointing out that it is forbidden to flush pets down the lavatory.

And there are fates worse than death. They will be forced to watch flamenco dancing and glass-blowing and ethnic juggling, they will be taken on four-hour coach trips to see Virgil's possible birthplace, or disappointingly thin waterfalls, or rocks bearing a faint resemblance to lions, they will be tethered outside folk museums and ruined castles, where local youths will chuck pebbles at them, they will be trodden on in teeming souks, they will be dragged up to the top of leaning towers and down to the bottom of niffy catacombs, they will lie panic-stricken on the floors of lurching cable-cars and pitching gondolas. And that is just the summers: pets hapless enough to belong to the wintersporting will annually face the prospect of ear-length snow and death by ski.

A passport to all this? It shouldn't happen to a dog.

# Grim Raper

Exactly 44 years ago, in May 1956 – and, by unsettling coincidence, exactly 44 years after the resonant couplet was first jotted, in May 1912 – I sat down with the school library's *Selected Poems of Rupert Brooke* to revise for an imminent Eng Lit A-level, and had just got dug into *The Old Vicarage, Grantchester*, when my spade struck stone, jarring the forearms so brutally that I can feel it yet. Because a wag, as so often happens with old school texts, had been there before me, and had left behind, with just one tiny downward stroke, only pencilled but inera-dicably subversive, the emendation: "Unkempt about those hedges blows / An English unofficial nose."

After that, I was never able to read the poem again without the image bursting back into my head – elbowing aside all Brooke's own, and rather more felicitous, images – of the young Apollo, golden-haired, plagued perhaps by hayfever, perhaps by a nostrilled greenfly insniffed from the original rose itself, honking helplessly into his red-spotted bandanna, his flowing locks shaken into kemptlessness as he reeled among the briars, while, at the reverberant blast, startled linnets evacuated every hedge within a half-mile radius, and church clocks stopped dead.

Now, why, this new morning, should I suddenly recall a moment from that ancient one? Because, an hour or so ago, I was strolling along the pavement beside the A41, that great trunk road invaluably connecting Cricklewood with Birkenhead, taking my daily 15-minute constitutional – not much of a constitutional perhaps, but then mine isn't much of a constitution – when I suddenly spotted, down in the grass verge among the more familiar crop of beer cans, fag packets, hub-caps, plastic bags, tissues, burger cartons, and all the rest of the wild urban flora which our caring Environment Secretary has done so much to conserve, a clump of oilseed rape blooms, tall, yellow, fluttering and dancing in the traffic-breeze, and so patently unofficial that Rupert Brooke's conk sprang instantly to mind. You know what I did next. I lowered my own, and sniffed.

Not bad at all. Though marinated in diesel and irrigated by dog, the flowers still succeeded in giving off that authentic rural whiff all too rare, notwithstanding its bucolic name, in Cricklewood. And because I wanted to give Mrs Coren a whiff of it, too, I not only sniffed, I plucked. Just the one bloom, of course: for, who knew, if the clump burgeoned, if the verge filled, if the flourishing spread, if profit beckoned, might farming not return to Cricklewood, long fields of barley and of rye, haywains, lowing herds, jolly yokels, buxom milkmaids, morris dancing, prize pigs, thatched Tescos?

However, when, five excited minutes later, I arrived home, Mrs Coren did not sniff. Mrs Coren shrieked. She does not shriek often. That is because I do not often bring home something which Mrs Coren is immediately able to identify as coming from God knows where, no, not the A41, I do not mean the A41, what I am asking is where was it before it got to the A41, it might have come bloody miles, you do not have the faintest idea where it blew here from, got carried in tyre tracks from, fell off a person from, got dropped by a bird from, I am not just talking about the farm it might have started out at which you know nothing about, it could well have originated in Canada, why are you looking at me like that, don't you read your own newspaper, don't you know that even as Nick Brown and Tim Yeo are at one another's throats, Baroness Young of English Nature is snapping at their heels because 30,000 British acres were planted with GM-contaminated oilseed rape imported from Canada, what do you mean you'll chuck it away then, it's a bit late to chuck it away, you have already come up the path waving it, it could be pollinating the hydrangeas right now, it could be blowing about all over the wistaria, it could even be . . .

Mrs Coren, it seemed, did not share my bright agricultural scenario, she had her own dark biotechnical one. Where I had heard only the morning horn of the

Cricklewood Hunt and seen the steaming brass-hung shire horses straining up Edgware Road and smelt the new-mown hay of Hendon, she had heard only the squelch of an abominable modification finally freeing itself from what had once been a rosebed and seen its tentacles effortlessly flail off our midnight door and smelt, wafting up the stairs, the unmistakable breath of a hungry triffid.

And, since she may well get around to reading this, I have to say that she could be right. Now that there is some corner of an English field that is for ever foreign, it might be wise, when the gong summons us to future teas, not to go anywhere near the honey.

# The Best Things In Life Are Free

As a major commentator whose finger is ever on the public pulse, I have to say, this morning, that I have rarely felt that pulse to be clattering so fast or so arrhythmically. The public is clearly having a bit of a turn. The public is in a cardiac tizz. So let me see if I can help: if you bend your fretful head and sniff the finger on your pulse, you will detect the fragrance of sandalwood. Yesterday, you would have smelt kelp. Try it tomorrow, and it could be peony, or musk. And since you surely know, after all these years, that I am not a man to fork out good money on silly smells, you should instantly conclude, with some relief, that I did not pay for all these soaps. I came by them.

And what you now want to know is whether I came by them honestly. For the reason you are so discombobulated is that you cannot get out of your head the vision of Mr and Mrs Kevin Mulgrew of Oldham being burst in upon at their own fireside by Greater Manchester Police, carried off by paddy wagon, and banged up for seven hours on suspicion that they had nicked a bedsheet from the RoadChef Lodge where they had just spent the sort of idyllic night that only Watford Gap can offer. But although the Mulgrews were completely innocent, the bedsheet having never left the motel and Greater Manchester Police having proved only that they are in fact Smaller Manchester Police, you the public remain deeply shaken. For you have been remembering all the bits and bobs which you yourselves have removed from hotel rooms over the years, and you have never really been sure that what you did wasn't criminal. Any moment now, you fear, your splintered door could allow entry to dog teams trained to sniff out titchy shampoo bottles and sachets of Earl Grey, detectives warranted to examine ballpoint pens for telltale logos and forage in biscuit barrels for unauthorised HobNobs, forensic boffins able to establish the true provenance of emery boards and cottonbuds, all of them keen to offer you a six-month break at one of the many snug hostelries belonging to the nationwide HMP chain.

Fear not. While it is of course a major offence to make

off with unused items provided by a generous hotel management, the seasoned traveller learns to avoid chokey by a few simple stratagems. Always remember that it is not a crime to leave with something for which the hotel could have no further use: if, for example, you tear off the neat little V with which all hotels sign their fresh lavatory rolls, the rest is yours by right, so that, after a fortnight's stay, you may legitimately pack 14. Lay beside them the 14 shower caps you never used because you took only baths, but be sure to pluck one hair to put in each. When requesting a new box of Kleenex every day, sneeze into the phone and talk thickly. You may also ask housekeeping for a new sewing kit daily, provided you throw one of the buttons of each out of the window. A note in the bedside drawer thanking the Gideon Society for your sudden conversion will allow you to keep the Bible.

A good way to both eat and collect chocolates is to ring room service each night and answer the door with a chocolate in your ear, saying you hadn't noticed it on the pillow. You may then eat the one from your ear and legitimately pack the other. A fake verruca will also enable you to collect 14 pairs of complimentary slippers, on medical grounds; just as a forged letter from your dentist saying you have unusually big teeth should produce 14 free tubes of Colgate's. It goes without saying that, on unpacking at home, you should squeeze each tube into a convenient tub, just in case the staff begin to ask themselves whether your teeth really did look bigger than normal and call the police. On reflection, it is probably wiser to ask for daily toothpaste on the grounds that you are addicted to sugar, especially since this will explain why your breakfast sugar bowl is always empty when the waiter comes to collect the tray. A used sock, which chambermaids are unlikely to feel, will hold up to one kilo of sugar lumps. The partner sock may be used to store packets of biscuits you do not wish legitimately to eat on the premises, but do remember to take a bite out of one per packet as soon as you get home.

As for soap, sniff my finger again. I have over 300 bars left, some dating back to 1973, each of them used just once.

# Bourgeois of the World Unite!

YOU will, I know, have been as intrigued as I to read the announcement from China that, as part of next year's commemoration of the 25th anniversary of the death of Chairman Mao, a new edition of his *Little Red Book* is to be issued, containing hitherto unpublished thoughts showing him to have been very much closer to China's current liberal and Western ideological positions than anyone had ever realised. I, indeed, was so intrigued that I immediately rang Beijing to ask the great man's literary executor to fax me a few typical extracts from what, he tells me, is to be called *The Second Thoughts of Chairman Mao*...

If there is to be a revolution, there must be a revolutionary party. Without a party built on Marxist-Leninist revolutionary theory and in the Marxist-Leninist revolutionary style, it is impossible to lead the broad masses of the people in defeating imperialism and its running dogs. The first thing, therefore, is to design a Marxist-Leninist tie.

Every Communist should grasp the truth that political power grows out of the barrel of a gun. Once he has paid for the gun, however, let him feel free to start saving for a snooker table.

We must have faith in the masses and the masses must have faith in the Party. These are two cardinal principles. The masses must believe that the Party is in a position to provide best fitted shagpile at factory prices, to include rubber underlay and making good, and the Party must believe that the masses will have the sense not to let the dog in.

Letting a hundred flowers blossom is the policy. Also putting a stone heron down by the azaleas and trimming the hedge to look like a teapot. And let all workers remember that, if there is space, a water feature sets things off a treat.

Who are our enemies? Who are our friends? These two questions are of prime importance for the revolution. Another one is where can we get those shirts with little crocodiles on?

Classes struggle, some classes triumph, other classes are eliminated. Such is history. To interpret history from this viewpoint is historical materialism; opposition to this viewpoint is historical idealism. Classes with inside plumbing have the best chance.

140

Whoever wants to know a thing has no way of doing so except by coming into contact with it. All genuine knowledge originates in direct experience. The worker would be wise, therefore, to ask for seven days' free trial and money back if not completely satisfied. A worker cannot be happy if his smoking jacket pinches under the arms, his compact discs crackle, his electric toothbrush rotates the wrong way, or spare ribs keep jamming his waste disposal.

No political party can possibly lead a great revolutionary movement to victory unless it has a revolutionary theory, a knowledge of history, and an annual Christmas Dance & Tombola (8 for 6.30, Black Tie).

Self-criticism must always be supported by mutual criticism. That is the path to victory. If a worker grows dissatisfied with his new deodorant, let him, before embarking upon any major decision, offer himself for a communal sniff.

A firm people and a firm party are welded together by a firm press. A firm press cannot exist without a lot of firm young women with nothing on, and plenty of firm scratchcards.

As for people who are politically backward, Communists should not slight or despise them, but befriend them, unite with them, convince them, and encourage them to go forward. For example, why not try to get an unsecured loan out of a Zurich bank manager?

Taught by mistakes and setbacks, we have become wiser. Once a mistake is made, we should correct it, and the more quickly and thoroughly the better. Thus, never mix radial tyres with cross-ply, never buy a loft extension from a man with an unmarked van, never back second favourites for a place, and always pocket your Rolex when entering a dark alley.

Thousands upon thousands of martyrs have heroically laid down their lives for the people. Let us hold their banner high and march ahead along the path crimson with their blood, confident that they would see nothing wrong in flying business class.

# The Stars Look Down

ONCE upon a not so distant time, I would, if the night was clear, amble out into my dewy garden, stare up at a million twinkling dots until my head spun, and be struck by how very insignificant they were. They were just dots. There was no intelligent life out there: nobody was writing *Martin Chuzzlewit* or tussling with the square root of minus one, nobody was bowling reverse swing to a legside trap or singing *My Old Man's a Dustman*, nobody was building Southend Pier out of lolly-sticks or threatening a black bishop with two white rooks. Twinkle though they might, the dots were dim. An Earth worm was smarter.

Not any longer. If I go out into my midnight garden now and stare up, there are a lot of very smart dots staring back. They not only twinkle, a lot of them move, and as they move they get smarter and smarter. They learn things. Some of them learn a billion things a night, because they can see at night, and every night they learn something new. On Sunday night, for example, they learnt that I had a blue shirt and drank gin. On Monday night, they found out about my red sweater and my cigar. Nor do they keep what they have learnt to themselves. They pass it on. They tell everyone. I do not feel smug about the dots any more. I feel uneasy.

Did you pluck your buckshee CD-Rom off the front of your *Sunday Times* last weekend? Did you spot that it had been produced in conjunction not only with the British National Space Centre, of which you had probably heard, but also with the Remote Sensing Society, of which you had probably not? And were you not perhaps slightly unsettled to discover that what this society was remotely sensing was you? For the CD-Rom, once you have poked it into your PC and poked your postcode into your keyboard, empowers you to see your satellite-spied backyard; poke someone else's code in, and you can see theirs. "And soon," gurgles the ecstatic newspaper, "it will be possible not only to pinpoint everybody on the planet, but also to see exactly what they are doing."

Um. How odd that bustling apple-cheeked Tony Poppins – who, as you know, is about to tell the rag trade to employ fatter catwalkers in order to prevent emulative teenagers going skinny – has not dragged the Remote Sensing Society into the nursery for a spoonful of cod-liver oil and a smack-bottom. But it is too late now: this is the end of society as we know it, because society as we know it is now utterly known. Oh, look, the woman from number 23 is hurrying up the path of number 36 and unlocking the front door. Why does she have a key? Oh, look, the man from number 36 is drawing his bedroom curtains. Oh, look, a Harrods van has arrived at number 14 and given a brown envelope to a man who is now burying it in his rockery, oh look, the couple from number 9 are harvesting their cannabis crop, the dog from number 12 has been thrown over the fence to eat the cat from number 10, the tip-up truck outside number 17 has just debouched a dozen illegal immigrants down the coal-hole, and as for that milkman who used to be Doris . . .

Not, mind, that our imminent conversion into a planet of Peeping Toms is what most bothers me, since I am an upright man with nothing to hide; what most bothers me is what lies in store for the nothing I have to hide, because it will put me on a hiding to nothing when commercial interests, as they inevitably will, get into the picture. Suppose that picture is of the nothing on top of my head? How long before I receive a letter from Rugs 'R' Us saying: "Dear Mr Coren, as a slaphead you should be considering something from our fine range, such as curly, grizzled, or the ever-popular ginger. As we have downloaded your MasterCard number, we are sending a boxful for your selection, money back if they blow off." Or: "Dear Mr Coren, we note that your roof and guttering have not had a finger on them in years, we have taken a small deposit out of your bank account and will be up your way Wednesday," or: "Dear Mr Coren, what is a prominent man like you doing with a ten-year-old banger, we have surfed the Net and learnt that Cowboy Pools plc are convinced from your building society account that you can definitely afford their Hollywood Mini-Kidney Plus Springboard, it would look a treat where your dead rosebed currently is, they

144

expect to start digging the hole any day now, but our view is you would be better off spending the money on a new Mercedes, it will easily fit into that garage of yours once you have moved the 28 old chairs, on three of the nine times we scanned your premises your wife was going on about it."

Twinkle, twinkle, little star, how I wonder what you are.

# One Spies With One's Little Eye

ALL those of us who, along with God, bless the Prince of Wales, and pray, apart from God, that his troubled life will henceforth be one of unblemished bliss, were transfixed by a sentence in Monday's *Times*. Embedded in a report of the Prince's recent nine-day visit to Scotland accompanied by Camilla Parker Bowles, the sentence concerned the further accompaniment by a third party, namely the Queen. What transfixed us about it was its revelation that she wasn't namely at the time. "She travelled secretly to stay for several days at the Craigowan Lodge on the Balmoral estate, in order to watch her son's progress at close hand."

Secretly? Does a newshound's ear not immediately

prick up? Does he not immediately ring Buck House for amplification, and upon having that ear filled with fleas, immediately prick up his newshound's nose? I was round at Euston station in a trice, waving my news-hound's chequebook, and it thus took only a trice or two more to nail a porter who told me that, yes, he did recall one recent passenger on the Aberdeen sleeper, a short kilted gentleman with a thick black beard who had asked him, in an unsettlingly shrill soprano, if one could tell one where one's berth was. You remember passengers like that, said the porter, especially when they explain that one cannot tip one because one never carries money.

Back home, I phoned Buck House again, and they caved in at once. This time, they filled my ear with facts. You do not often get exclusives in this slot, dear readers, but you have one now. Upon arrival, at Aberdeen station, it seems, Her Majesty hired a white Avis van, removed her beard, and drove the 45 miles to Craigowan Lodge to establish her presence, telling staff she did not wish to be disturbed; only, an hour or so later and with a kitbag of assorted props, to leave by the laundry chute and drive the van south to Holyroodhouse, where her son and his paramour were staying. Changed, in the back of the van, into dungarees, blacked up with Cherry Blossom and carrying a plumber's bag, the Queen then marched to the gate, announced, in an evidently credible Tobagan accent, that one had come about the smell on the landing, man, gave a high-five to the Master of The Queen's Drains, and disappeared upstairs. It was there, in a tiny attic room, that she lodged for the next nine days, emerging only in a variety of remarkable disguises, with the sole purpose of assessing not her son's progress at all, but Mrs Parker Bowles, as intimately yet as covertly as possible. Banging, for example, on her boudoir door one afternoon, concealed behind a yashmak cleverly consonant with her notional status as a Balkan refugee, the Queen was in a unique position to observe the generosity of a woman who, though virtually hyphenated, was only too ready to fork out for two dishcloths and a luminous key-ring. That this largesse was complemented by a commendable frugality, was, according to my exclusive Palace source, amply borne out when the Queen, observing her quarry through a knothole in the airing cupboard of the laundry room, saw her reclaiming the left leg from one pair of tights and the right leg from another, both of whose partners had laddered, and sewing them together to form a serviceable new pair – something, Her Majesty confided to my informant, which would have done credit to the legendarily careful George V.

And the next day, watching from the garage block where, in her toque and handlebar moustache, Her Majesty was ostensibly taking a fag break from her kitchen duties, she spotted Camilla about to drive off for a morning shop, and was hugely impressed by the fact that she checked her mirror before engaging first gear. Better yet, the Queen was quite overwhelmed when, having quick-changed into a meter-maid's uniform, tracked down her quarry to a parking bay off Princes Street, and slapped a ticket on her windscreen, she found that the returning driver did not abuse the Queen or pull her hair, but sweetly informed her she was only doing her job, and gave her a Glacier Mint. It is possible, of course, that Camilla was merely taking pity on a woman with a handlebar moustache, but even this invites a favourable construction.

Certainly, that must be how the Queen interpreted it, and everything else she saw during those nine detective days. Why else would she, last Saturday, agree to attend the Highgrove barbecue, publicly meeting Mrs Parker Bowles for the first time? As a caring mother, she has patently eased her qualms. Whether, mind, that is enough to persuade her soon to become a caring mother-in-law, my source – close and authoritative though he may have been – was not prepared to guess.

# Funky Gibbons

THOSE of you who happened to fetch up at page 26 of Monday's *Times* will, I know, have been struck by the headline: "Stanley Gibbons to split from Flying Flowers". I also know that you will have been struck in many different ways, for it is that kind of headline: some of you, for example, will have rolled your eyes over your cornflakes – not, I hope, too literally – and groaned at yet another celebrity rift, for Stan Gibbons was doubtless some billionaire midfield star to whose Phuket tryst with the jetsetting lead singer of the billionaire Flower Girls an entire issue of *Hello!* had, only a few short months back, been devoted, with the predictable consequence that he had now decamped with her scatty pseudo-sibling, Wild Flowers. Unless, of course, the boot was on the other foot and Flying Flowers was instead the lightning Welsh fly-half whose long-term partner, decor icon Stanley Gibbons, had flounced out in fury after a tabloid doorstepped the couple to reveal not only that none of the Flowers grandparents had even visited Wales, but also that the love nest's pelmets clashed horribly with the futon.

Then again, might the Flying Flowers not be a daredevil aerobatic team whose swashbuckling leader, Stanley Gibbons, having recently gargled too many free samples of his sponsors' best bitter, looped the loop for six straight hours before parachuting fuellessly into the Solent, leaving the great brewers no option but to demand his immediate resignation?

Sadly, no: the headline referred to none of the above, for page 26 was in the Business News, and in dull reality Stanley Gibbons is the famous philatelic business and Flying Flowers the famous floral business. And what is sad about the split is that when they merged two years ago, my heart leapt, but now they are splitting, it has sunk. For, throughout those years, that heart has been going pit-a-pat in anticipation of the merger's first fruit: I had been awaiting *The Stanley Gibbons Flower Catalogue*, for it would have made me rich and famous. Top collectors from all over the world would have flocked to my garden to goggle and spend. Now, that might baffle regular readers, since this column has frequently wept on your broad shoulders after this or that horticultural debacle, and the idea that my little brownfield site is now packed to the gunwales with exemplary flora will be hard to entertain. Do not even try: try only to recall your own childhood poring over *The Stanley Gibbons Stamp Catalogue*, in which everything that was perfect was worthless. Blemishes were where the big money was: for tuppence, you could buy enough Hungarian footballers of such size, variety and painterly virtue as to enable you to paper the Sistine ceiling without anyone cottoning on, but if what you wanted was a torn Albanian scrap with King Zog's head on it upside down and atypically puce, you would first have to run into Barclays with a shotgun. Moreover, if a sloppy perforator had stitched his little holes down the middle of it instead of down the side, you would also have to run, having gutted Barclays, into Lloyds.

So you can see how excited I was when Stan went into the flower business. Stan knew a thing or two about the value of rarity. Take the remarkable khaki camellia, of which but one example remains, and that only just: there are millions of camellias, all identical to the one in the little picture tied to the shrivelled shank of mine, which is to say covered in bright red flowers, and none can be worth more than their original £19.95: what a true collector would be prepared to spend to get his hands on the only one which blossoms every year into little brown cobnuts, I cannot imagine. As for the unique Clematis Cricklewoodiae, which (thanks to some imponderable flaw in what I rather think is its only gene) does not climb walls, as all its common siblings do, but prefers to crawl slowly along the ground strangling any plant in its path – can Kew boast one? I think not. Nor, on my many visits there in search of some expert competent to explain why, when I sow seeds in my rockery, only rocks come up, have I ever spotted anything comparable to my Rosa nonfloribunda, a truly stunning example of symbiosis in that, instead of producing flowers, it produces little green animals which subsist entirely upon the mother plant. It may, mind, not be a uniquely aberrant rose at all, it could well be a Venus Fly Trap which has somehow got its dietary wires crossed, and is thus even more valuable.

But now Stanley is splitting, I shall never know. Whether I shall ever come to terms with the poignant – and costly – truth that full many a flower is born to rot unseen, only time will tell.

# A Tough One To Crack

WERE Humpty Dumpty to have a great fall today, it would do him no harm at all. Concerned bystanders would not fish frantically for their mobiles to call upon the services of all the king's horses and all the king's men – mind you, it has always puzzled me why they were ever invited to put him together in the first place, given that surgery is not what a horse is good at – for Humpty Dumpty would simply shake himself, nod reassuringly to the bystanders, and get back on the wall. Something else which has always puzzled me, as a matter of fact, given that climbing is not what an egg is good at.

You can see that I know a lot about eggs. For which, by the end of today's little folderol, you will be extremely grateful, because Easter is almost upon us, and in order to enjoy it to the full you will need to know some of what I know. Not all of it, nobody needs to know all that: you do not need to know, for example – though it would appear you are about to – that there is something called the Poultry Club. I do not know everything about the Poultry Club, as it was shut when I phoned, possibly because fowl, clapped out by seasonal demand, take a long Easter break, so I have not actually visited its premises to see the chickens sitting around in brown leather *fauteuils*, clucking over the editorials in *Poultry World* as they sip a large worm-and-tonic, but I certainly intend to ring them again, once they re-open, if only to find out under what circumstances they allow un-accompanied hens to eat in the cockerels' dining room.

And yes, I know about *Poultry World* because I rang them, too; they were the ones who put me on to the Poultry Club. And I was put on to *Poultry World* by the British Egg Industry Council, which the Ministry of Agriculture, Fisheries and Food put me on to. It took a long time for them to do it, mind, since if you phone MAFF, you are connected to an android helpline which insists on telling you all about passports for pets, and you have to listen to this for some hours until a live operator comes on and tells you that nobody there does eggs – unless, I suppose, you have a pet egg and wish to take it abroad, I didn't ask. The operator did, however, say that the British Egg Industry Council knew about eggs. Well, they would. But they didn't: at least, they didn't know what I wanted to know.

You would think, wouldn't you, that someone in all this ovular lot would know why eggs have tougher shells than they used to? That's why I rang MAFF in the first place: I had recently grown aware that my three-minute eggs were coming up sloppier than before, that it took several thwacks with a knife to find this out (when all my life I had been able to decapitate them with a single deft stroke of which Jack Ketch would have been proud), and that if you wanted to fry rather than boil them, you now had to bang eggs on the edge of the pan until it dented.

I wanted, in short, to know whether contemporary eggs were growing thicker, tougher shells. It seemed an innocent enough inquiry, but either none of the top eggies knew, or, for some reason, weren't saying; I found myself wondering whether they had perhaps been put on the back foot by all the shenanigans over listeria and salmonella and were now keeping publicly mum but reporting inquiries like mine to Egg I 5, who might very well dispatch an agent to waylay and scramble me, but I couldn't prove anything. So I gave up and went out for a late breakfast, and the chef – chef? – at the Cricklewood Diner said, bloody right, they're like bullets, these days. I was going to ask him whether his huge forearms had been developed by all that cracking, but they sported these somewhat aggressive tattoos, so I didn't push it.

And when I got home, I found an answerphone message from something called the British Egg Information Service. I don't know how they got my phone number, there is probably an Ova Nostra network, but I steeled myself against the possibility of getting a kiss of death blown into the earpiece or finding a chicken's head in my bed, and rang back. They wanted to know why I wanted to know if eggs had tougher egg-shells, and I said I just wanted to know, and there was a pause, but finally she said, all right, yes, some do. And before I could ask why, she rang off.

Do you see how hard I have been working on your behalf? You now know what I know: that, for a happier Easter, your three-minute eggs should be boiled for four, and eggs for frying should be opened with a cleaver. And if, on your way to church, you hear that I have been found in an alley with an egg-filled sock lying mysteriously beside my corpse, say a little prayer for me.


# *Four Eyes Good*


THOUGH not, perhaps, a household name wherever revisionist historians foregather (and who would wish to be, these days?), I have never been one to recoil from controversial reinterpretation should fresh evidence turn up. And it has. It has been turned up by the eminent trowel of Dr Magnus Sundstrom, who, poking about in Gotland recently, found what have just been confirmed, by no less an ophthalmological whiz than Dr Olaf Schmidt of Aalen University, as Viking spectacles. "We were amazed," Schmidt yelled at the *Daily Mail*, "that the principles they used to make these lenses were not understood until centuries later, yet these people still managed to create something with an optical quality comparable with that of modern glasses!"

Might it not be time, then, to reach for our own and take a fresh look at what we may well conclude have ever been a grossly maligned people? I am not an invasion denier, I do not dispute that, a millennium ago, the Vikings rowed here in tooled-up droves and gave our hapless forebears a serious hammering; I seek only to wonder whether there might not be an emollient explanation for what the British have always regarded as the totally unacceptable behaviour of brutal oiks.

Let us begin by considering eighth-century Scandinavia before the Vikings went anywhere. It is now clear to me that nothing was clear to them: the Vikings did not go anywhere because they could not see where they were going. This also explains why they all wore the same hats. Had they all worn different hats, it would have been impossible for these myopic folk, at the end of a drunken mead-hall evening, to select their own hat from the hat-stand. It is also why their hats had big horns, since there is no reason to have big horns on your hat except to make it easier to find if you're short-sighted. You can feel for it. However, the Vikings were a deeply serious people – they did, after all, end up as Danes – and, unable to go anywhere, sensibly employed the time saved by not going anywhere in working out how to see better. After a bit, they invented spectacles. They could now see everything. They soon discovered that the noisy wet stuff they had been constantly stumbling into went on for miles, and that the big things that hurt your face were trees. Now that they could see, they were in a position to chop down the big things without losing a finger, and build boats to sail on the wet stuff. They could go places.

Which is how they arrived in Britain. Unquestionably, they came in peace, because generations of not being able to make anything out clearly would discourage war: you never knew whom you might kill, foes, friends, selves, when waving swords so huge they could be lifted only with two hands. We now know, of course, why the swords were so big. Like the hats. Our invaded ancestors, however, did not know this: all they saw was creatures with huge horns and glass eyes running up the beach dragging enormous swords. Understandably, the Britons would have fled. The Vikings would have rushed after them, burst into their huts bellowing amicable explanations in a language the Britons did not understand, the panicked Britons would have lashed out desperately, and large numbers of spectacles would have been knocked off.

So that the Vikings were now short-sighted again. They would have begun flailing about in the huts trying to find their glasses, but smashing all the bits and bobs the Britons owned. What we now unjustly describe as pillage was, in fact, rummage. As to what we now unjustly describe as rape, I am strongly disposed to believe that this should enjoy the same optical exculpation: Vikings whose glasses had broken would not have known whether they were grappling with men or women, and when it comes to grappling, one thing can easily lead to another. As for Vikings whose glasses were not broken, it is quite possible that our female ancestors either laughed at them or took them for wimps, most probably both, and that the deeply insulted invaders, fearful of the damage likely to be done to a Scandinavian reputation for efficient nookie which persists to this day, responded with what was in truth nothing more than an excusably patriotic attempt to keep the flag flying. There is also the possibility that some Vikings, even more optometrically sophisticated than the rest, were crawling about on all fours, trying to find their contact lenses, when panicking female Britons inadvertently got under them, giving further currency to the malicious calumnies from which these luckless Magoos suffered for so long, until Dr Sundstrom's fortuitous dibbling at last enabled me to set the historical record straight.

# I Blame the Dealers

THE report in yesterday's *Times* that Pietro Forquet, Italy's most venerated bridge master, had, during Friday's national championships, been tested for drugs, will have stunned players the world over. Not because, as non-players might jump to conclude, bridge is the very last game in which drugs could play a significant part, but because, as every player knows, it is the very first.

What point was there in testing Signor Forquet for substances so integral to the game since the dawn of bidding that, without them, it can never properly be played at all?

Let us illustrate this with a hand played in the opening match of last weekend's Cricklewood Championships. North, South (Mrs North), East, and West (Mrs East) have begun the evening with their narcotics of choice, large dry martinis, straight up, no twist, and have now sat down at the card table – East somewhat heavily, with the result that the table lurches, spilling their pencils on to the carpet. North, South and West glance sharply at East, who declares that the table must have a wobbly leg. West responds that it is not the table that has wobbly legs. North and South say nothing, but exchange a glance, noticeably irritating East, who suspects some tacit coded message. Each player now bends to retrieve his pencil but North, in straightening up, bangs his head on the corner of the table, to which South says Oh God, not you, too, North's response being What do you mean not me, too, at which East intervenes with Yes, what do you mean, not him, too, and West counters with You know what she means not him, too. North in emollient reply refills everyone's glass, deals, and opens one spade.

East passes, and South replies with I seem to have 14 cards. West says I have 11, North swears and says It's these cards, they're sticky, it must be the gin, and East says it's the gin all right, and now exchanges his own tacit coded message with West. After the reshuffle, North deals, again, goes white, and, before speaking, lights a cigarette. East says those are my fags, I thought you'd given up, which South answers with, yes he has, he is nervous, he has obviously got an amazing hand. North shouts Thank you, partner, shall I just tell them what I'm holding, has a coughing fit, and opens two clubs, indicating slam potential. East passes, and South responds with You're sweating, have you had your pill? West says What does he take, is it a beta-blocker, I didn't think they mixed with alcohol, whereupon East replies, They don't, it affects your judgement, he probably doesn't have a two-club opener at all, I bid two diamonds, to which North shouts that he can't do that, he has already passed, but East argues that he can, because South hasn't bid yet. North now brings his fist down on the table with such force that South's drink topples into her lap. She rushes out for a cloth, dropping her cards, face up, on to the table, thereby revealing more than enough points to have made the grand slam her partner invited.

While South is away, West pours herself another large one, and, grown consequently maudlin, stares at South's cards until the tears begin rolling down her cheeks. East says What is it now? and West sobs I never get cards like that, I never ever get good cards, to which West responds It wouldn't matter much if you did, and West howls What is that supposed to mean? and runs out, just as South returns, in a blouse and slacks, saying It may interest you to know that I have had to chuck that dress in the bin, it is ruined, whose deal is it, where the hell is West? In response, there is a thud and assorted tinkles from beyond the room, and, after some time, West shuffles unsteadily in. She is covered in earth and petals, and opens with You ought to do something about that rug, to which North responds What rug? encouraging the reply You know what bloody rug, the one that slides and could kill people, evoking South's intervention of How can it slide, it has that big Edwardian pedestal jardinière standing on it, the one my mother left me. West says Pass. South asks East what she means by Pass, is this some convention I haven't come across, and East responds you have now, it means there isn't a jardinière standing on it any more, look at the state of her.

It is at this point that the distraught West gropes frantically inside her handbag, leading North, South and East to conclude that she is looking for a mirror and make-up, but West is actually engaged in a sly finesse, since what she is really after is her Valium. Before anyone can intervene, she has popped four pills, washed them down with the remaining contents of the jug, and slumped face down on the table. East deals.

# *Godbye, Cricklewood, I Must Leave You*

IT is time for me to leave Cricklewood. I have no option. I do not want to leave Cricklewood, God knows (for He can see my fingers trembling as they tap the words, He can hear the hot tears pattering on to my keyboard, He understands, it is His job) but any day now – make that any night – I shall heartbrokenly chuck the bits and bobs of three decades aboard a handcart, grease its axle, muffle its wheels, and, provided there is no moon, push, literally, off. Praying as I furtively scuttle that there is no insomniac neighbour standing at his bedroom window keen-eyed enough, despite the dark, to speed my going with a valedictory brick. For who would blame him? These 30 years, he and his fellow-villagers have indulged me with an ever-lengthening tether, but now, at last, they have found themselves at the end of it.

Brought there by Richard Curtis. Because Richard Curtis, who lives in Notting Hill, has made a film called *Notting Hill*. I know I do not need to tell you this, I know you knew it two seconds after God knew it, for *Notting Hill*, though it has not even publicly opened, is the most known film ever made. Everything about it has been told in Gath and published in the streets of Askelon. Previews have appeared to shepherds watching their flocks by night. Open any Gobi tabloid, switch on any Inuit channel, cock an ear in any souk, down any coalmine, up any alp and the talk is of little else. There can be nobody on the planet who does not know that *Notting Hill* stars Hugh Grant as an unsuccessful bookseller who falls for a famous actress played by Julia Roberts, just as there can be nobody who has not read that, as the result of all this taradiddle, Notting Hill stands poised to shove *Casablanca* from its podium as celluloid's most glamorous address. It could well become the first nominee to win an Oscar for Best Postal District. So, since Mr Curtis has manifestly triumphed, by his myriad romanticing skills, in making this dog-eared West London enclave so chic, so famous, so globally desirable, is it any wonder that his neighbours should fall to their knees each bedtime, and bless his name?

And is it obversely any wonder that mine do not go to bed at all, preferring to hold black masses, strangle cockerels, and stick rusty hatpins into a crude plasticine mannikin with a snapshot snipped from *The Times* gummed to its little bald head so that Old Nick need be left in no doubt whatever? You would not believe the new *froideur* in the Cricklewood streets, crossed as soon as they spot me coming by those who would once smile, and pause, and gossip. Dogs are tugged away from my pat, children folded into their mothers' skirts, change is wordlessly slapped down on shop counters, and Next Window signs slapped up in banks and post offices. I have only to appear in pubs for darts games to finish and landlords to run out of ice, and every time I set foot on a zebra crossing I take my life in my hands. If I wanted to borrow a cup of sugar or a pair of secateurs, I should have to drive for miles.

So then, is this sudden and deeply distressing disaffection simply the product of Cricklewood's resentment that I have not done for it what Richard Curtis did for Notting Hill? Are the villagers enraged that the hack among them did not seize the chance to glorify their patch into an international byword for cuteness to fill the absent world with envy? Well yes, but that, I fear, is only a part of it. For it is not simply that, while Mr Curtis has sought every opportunity to select those features of Notting Hill which will enhance its charm and assiduously eschew those which might detract, I have, for Cricklewood, always striven to do the opposite, since my neighbours seem never to have minded that too much, have rarely raised a hackle, and have only occasionally tutted – perhaps because they were grateful that Cricklewood received any public mention at all, but certainly because they clearly never felt that any harm was being done. Then what has so upset them, now?

What has so upset them now is that brightest among all the glare of publicity attending *Notting Hill* shines the revelation that local property prices have gone through the roof of every house, flat, and kennel in the area – including Mr Curtis's own two-bedroom bolt-hole, currently on the market at £1.3 million. And that, I'm afraid, is what Cricklewood holds against me. It senses that my depiction of it down the long arches of the years will serve only to prove that prices can go down as well as up. That is why I shall have to leave; although quite when, of course, I cannot say. Selling my house won't be easy.

# *The Long Goodbye*

IF I shove up the sash of my loft window tonight, for the last time, and I risk my neck with fraying sashcord, for the last time, by poking my head out, for the last time, an ear to the nocturnal hum of Cricklewood, shall I hear, above that hum, the cheery song of a cockney ghost? Why not? She is, after all, just a couple of hundred yards away, and tonight is her cue, if any night ever was, for song. True, she has been silent in her grave, in the cemetary at the corner of my road, since 1922, but what of that? I shall hear Marie Lloyd singing, even if nobody else does.

Because she will be telling me not to dilly-dally on the way. And she is right: I shall not dilly-dally long. Just long enough to tell you, who have dallied here with me over the long years, that, an hour or so ago, off went the van with my home packed in it. I, however, did not walk behind with my old cock linnet, I stayed behind with my old cock typewriter, because I wanted this empty house to echo, for the last time, to the skeletal rattle of the old Remington boneshaker which took down my first Cricklewood communique, 28 years ago. I shall not pass it to you from there, mind, because a lot has happened in 28 years and newspapers do not take typescript any more; I shall, in a bit, pocket it, and go off to my nice new house, and transcribe it onto a computer which will phone it to *The Times*. I am not, if you are reaching for the Kleenex, doing this out of mawkishness; I am doing it because if I just went off and did it on my computer, I could not write about being in Cricklewood, since my computer is on the van, and when it gets out of the van, in an hour or so, it will not be in Cricklewood.

All right, pluck the Kleenex: I cannot fib to you, you know me too well, I am doing this partly out of mawkishness. Anyone leaving the house in which he has spent half his life will be a mawk. Do you, by the way, know what a mawk is? It is a maggot. At least, it was when Old Norsemen were naming things, but if you were pondering why this word should gradually have turned into what it means now, stop. Especially with Marie up the road, and with me feeling, tonight, a trifle mortal, too, and furthermore, sensing around me the ghosts – though sceptics among you are welcome to call them memories – of all those who have passed temporarily through this house during those 28 years, and have now passed permanently elsewhere.

If I look down into the garden from this open window, I can see them all on the lawn, drinking, talking, eating, laughing, sniffing the roses, plucking the raspberries, peering in the pond for fish, poking in the shrubbery for cricket balls, all that. It is, of course, pitch dark down there, so you wouldn't be able to see them, but I can. I can even see me, though it requires something of an effort to recognise him, because it is his first day in the garden: he is slim, he has hair, he has one child on his shoulders and one in his arms; a feat he would find a little tricky now, since, in a trice, both have become a mite more cumbersome.

I can hear the trees in the dark tonight, because there is a breeze. The slim hairy one garlanded with kids could have heard them, not because there was no breeze, then, but because there were no trees, except for the giant acacia in the middle of the lawn, the focus of my eye-line for 28 years every time that, stumped, I looked up from the daily keyboard. Could be, what, a million times? Two million? A lot of stumping has gone on, up here. But all the other trees – the maple, the cedar, the cherry, the chestnut, the beech, the hawthorn, the fig, the crab apple, the eucalyptus, the thugia, the pear, the photinia – came to the garden in little tubs, and most of them are higher than this loft, now, which is why the breeze is having such sussurant fun in them. It is probably having so much fun that some of the leaves are falling, though I cannot see them, because what I can do is sniff autumn on that breeze, not the best of scents for mawkies. We should have sold the house in the spring, but the trees looked so good, and the lawn so lush, and the plants so buddie, that we thought, okay, house, one last summer.

There is only one song about Cricklewood. The wizards in the BBC archives found it for me a few years back, when I was, as so often, banging on about the place for Radio 4. Its opening couplet runs: "Cricklewood, Cricklewood, you stole my life away/For I was young and beautiful, but now I'm old and gray." Not much of a song, perhaps, hardly one for Marie, but it'll do for me, tonight. It is time to close the typewriter and slip away. Tomorrow to fresh woods and crickles new.